It's Been One Hell of a Ride

Jump In, Grip Tight, and Enjoy!

Ride 1

Nikki—
may you see the humor, blessings
and lessons on your ride!

Jennifer
2·22·2020

By Jennifer Collins-Timm

PAGE PUBLISHING, INC.
Conneaut Lake, PA

First originally published by Page Publishing 2019

ISBN 978-1-64584-119-7 (pbk)
ISBN 978-1-64584-120-3 (digital)

Printed in the United States of America

To my Timm men, I love our story. I wanted to read our story, so I wrote our story. You helped make all my dreams come true!

Ride 1

It's Been One Hell of a Ride is a pretty sarcastic, totally true, and comical ride. A two-part book started as a journal of our family story to my Timm men. It's a book on how we began this ride. How we dealt with many life hiccups with humor. How we picked our battles and learned to breathe through the struggles. How we enjoyed the little things. Also, to remember the good times, remember the bad times, and to learn from it and move on. Keep trucking as this is your ride, and it's ultimately up to you to make it the best ride it can be!

In this creating process, it dawned on me that this book is not just for us but also for others. It's for all pondering their place on the path. It reassures all panickers this isn't going the way it was planned and that's okay. You just let the ride take you, learn to love it, and find the humor in it, as the grass really isn't greener over here or there. I'm sure many of you can relate that our rides have bumpy paths, but we always have the option to steer it in a different direction.

I'm game to share all, invite you into my world, and let you experience this Timm ride. Jump in, grip tight, and enjoy!

(Now if the judging and nasty snickers begin, please shut this book and step away. No ugly cows welcomed on this path. Greatly appreciated.) With that being said, here we go.

In the Beginning

Don't be afraid of being different. Be
afraid of being like everyone else!
—Unknown

From the earliest of memories, my mother tried to set me up on playdates with a girl from a block over. I, of course, put up a fight, not wanting this arranged friendship. Not because I didn't like the girl or found her completely annoying, but because I was quite content hanging with me, myself, and I. I didn't need any arranged friendship, especially by my mom—seriously (roll of the eyes). Nor did I want an arranged playdate to be tortured into enduring hours of playing kitchen or dolls. Jeez, did she not get me!

Full throttle ahead a few more years to a Collins' clan family get-together. While all the cousins were off digging in the creek, squishing their toes in the mud, chasing frogs, or doing God knows what else, I was just hanging back with the adults. Sitting on the picnic-table bench, feeling the soft summer breeze, and minding my own business when I heard my mother announce to the family, "She's a bit of a loner." (Yes, I heard it! I could hear then. Stay tuned for full gossip on my hearing.)

What the hell! Again, I was just chilling, taking in the peace. I was content to just *be*, and I get labeled with what sounded like the most hideous, negative with horns and a wart designation. It just sounded like my mother called me, in front of my whole family, a *loser*! How embarrassing. Where's the hole to curl up in? Where's the blanket to cover me? I know, I know, now. That's not what she said nor what she meant at all. But at the time, that's how I felt and how I associated the word *loner*. Can't one not have to be entertained, active, and surrounded by others their own age? To listen to their chatter all the time? But just be in the moment, alone in thought and content? Isn't that what most strive for?

Poor Mom, I'm not picking on her. Really, I'm not. She was trying, giving effort, trying to explain *me* to others. Trying to help me and encourage me and give me a little shove. I know this now, as I full steam ahead many years to what I am now doing with my own boys. Jeez, JennJenn, don't you get it? Just back off! (I've been called many things through the years; JennJenn is one of my most cherished names. My boys call me that. Everyone was "Mom" in public and every mom looked when it was yelled. I am hard of hearing, so the only way to get my attention was yelling JennJenn. I still go by that to my Timm men.)

In my early teen years, I remember clearly sitting on the counter in my bathroom. (Yes, my own bathroom. Well, I shared with my older brother, but I honestly don't remember him being around much. So yeah, I had my own bathroom.) I was just staring at myself in the bathroom mirror, wondering, pondering, and imagining what I would look like at seventeen, twenty, and twenty-five. Funny, I don't remember imagining past twenty-five. Was anything past twenty-five years of age ancient? I'm in my early forties now and still see me as that same gal from years ago, back in the mirror. Sure, with the addition of a few accented gray hairs, tastefully placed age spots, stressed rings around the eyes, and pillow-created crease lines on my face. Let's not discuss the scars or stretch marks strategically mapped out all over my body as well. But I'm still *me*. It shocks me when I hear the grocery checkout twerp call me ma'am. Who, *moi*?

By my mid-teens I had changed social groups from the what some small-town folks may consider as the popular crowd over to the "march to our own beat" skater crew and was embraced with a huge "get over here, girl" welcome. It was also followed with a sense of "just be you"—finally! The mask could come off, the pressure was lifted, and the ulcer that was brewing in my tummy fizzled. I didn't have to try to fit in. I could be me. The similar interests, choice of peculiar clothing, the "not giving a rat's ass" attitude, maybe even the mood swings and the odd conversations brought a level of creativity and stellar plans for the future.

As a hormonal teen, life was turbulent. As a lost soul, I was drawn to others just as lost. Maybe it was the mysterious way of us. Maybe it was the attention that we got from others or lack of attention. We were explosive all together, and that fueled our unstable behavior. But boy, did we have fun and were together all the time. Maybe a few friendships were fueled by the "you can't tell me what to do or who to be with" attitude.

Never once did those earlier year visions entertain the plans for a traditional mapped-out path of state college (I want my own path), marriage (the old ball and chain), mortgaged home (feeling stuck), a neighborhood setting (June Cleaver, I so am not), children (I can barely take care of me, nor can I cook), and an eight-to-five office job (beating my head against a wall). For me, the big plan was to escape my small hometown and go off to a true art school, explore city museums and plays, backpack across Europe, save adorable pathetic-looking dogs, and have my own creations sold in businesses and at shows. Just one big "Zen Jenn's amazing adventure."

Before I knew it, the day of high school graduation had arrived. My bags were packed, ready to be on my way to the first stop of an area community college with a few from my skater crew. My mom was firm that each of us three kids started summer college classes soon after high school graduation, so we weren't around to get in trouble all summer. Really, us Collins kids? Fine. I guess it was a good plan and possibly easier on her for the goodbyes and not dragging it out. After a few portfolio submissions and sit-in illustration days, I was invited into their commercial art program. We were told on orientation day that usually only 50 percent of the starting class would make it to graduation day. Booyah! This gal made it there and ended second in her class! The next step *was* to cruise on to an art school in Minneapolis. That was my plan.

As luck had it, something better was put on my path. As part of the new plan, my man disreputably jumped in my path—or more like dived head-on to get this distracted gal's attention! Remember, I wasn't one of those girls who sat around dreaming of family and marriage, a house, scheduled days, color coordinating a calendar, living by the clock at an office job, a management title, or sports on weekends. That wasn't part of the vision. And yet this new plan was set in motion, as crazy and wild as it was.

You see, there are all roads to travel. They are there to explore. It may not be part of your original game plan and you can always head back into the original direction. But maybe, just maybe, a new path could be a bit more exciting than you ever imagined. Get out of your comfort zone for once and view for yourself!

You Are My Sackin' Fish

A "sackin' fish" is the one you keep—
the one you don't toss back.
—my great-grandma Betty,
a.k.a. Grandma Grape

I worked part-time at a large, nationwide contract-supply store in the paint department while attending community college. It was fitting for me, as my dad was a contractor and first started out his career as a house painter. I remember my manager at the time pointing down the aisle to this white-pants, crisp-collared, tucked-in shirt, clean haircut, freshly shaven guy standing over a stocking pallet, laughing and talking with his coworkers: "That is the new assistant manager. He starts next week." Hmm, okay, whatever. On with my business. And the adventure begins!

Quickly after this clean, crisp, white pants-wearing assistant manager was in the paint department, I found myself scheduled on his shift a lot. We seemed to find ourselves in the same aisle, striking up conversations often. It was a bit annoying; remember, I like quiet, space, and am quite content with me, myself, and I. Sometimes he came across a bit cocky with his advice: "When the paneling starts to fall, you should move." Yes, I know this now, lesson learned. This white-pants, clean cut, tucked-in shirt, "tell it how it is" assistant manager turned out to be my sackin' fish! My great-grandma Betty warned of it years ago. "Wait for your sackin' fish." Don't settle; be patient. Your sackin' fish is out there. My Ryan threw out a speed bump on my "pedal to the metal," rugged road joyride that I was on.

Opposites do attract. This man was my shock factor to my family and, up to then, friends. Still is, twenty-plus years later, even to me. I questioned this pairing a few times through the years. But I realize fully now that he is my man who has made this amazing, wild, crazy ride all possible. He is the man who guided me through and stepped back to let me be me; and I wouldn't be the real me without his patience, sarcasm, help, and humor. With his often "what the hell is wrong with you" wink or smile.

When you know it, you know it. Six months after meeting we moved in together. I mean really, he was always in my space anyway. A year after we met, he proposed in typical Ryan style—short and to the point. Nine months later, I graduated from community college and was hired on full-time at a large insurance corporation as a desktop publisher because I was top of my class and determined to be on my way. Two weeks later, we were married in a traditional church wedding back in my hometown, in a big tulle princess dress my mother had made (now *that* whole scenery is a "what the hell" moment). Great, this is how it spins out from here. I never did make it to Minneapolis for art school. Why did I need to? I had a full-time job and a man on my arm who, coincidentally, was originally from Minnesota. So in a way plans were having high-five connections, right?

I married a guy who has truly been my best friend. He gives me a shoulder to cry on, arms to lean into after a bad day, space when needed, hands to hold, flowers me with attention, harsh, cold, to-the-point words when necessary, laughs, and more laughs. He hands me a large glass of wine when needed, greets with coffee in bed, provides a cooked meal every day—because seriously, we *all* know I'm not going to dazzle in that room. I envision that area could easily be turned into a cool sitting room with a hammock, but that earned me another "what the hell is wrong with you" wink. He lets me be *me*. My Ryan is truly awesome. He's a tea-making, back-rubbing, steam-mopping, chick-flick-getting kind of man! Do you want to puke yet? Hold it back. There's more to read.

My Ryan has a very simple tell-it-how-it-is approach to everything, especially in his remarks on life. And yes, after a long time, I have come to feel the same way:

Don't know, don't care.
Who cares what others think. We all have our own opinions.
I'm not saying, but I'm just saying...

At first, I have to admit, I found it cold and a bit cocky. Now I find it refreshing. You know where you stand with Ryan. Accept it and move on. No sugarcoating from this guy.

"Four hundred million dollars, baby" was and seems to still be his response each and every time I ask what something costs. I don't always know what items or services cost us because that is his response, period. Always. Now you know in the cosmic world they say if you think, dream, or concentrate on something long enough it shall happen. Therefore, I do see this 400 million dollars appearing to us someday, *or* he's had it all along and doing some sick, twisted test to see if I would stick with him through it all without his very padded golden money tree. That would be my Ryan!

One of the things I just adore is seeing elderly couples walking hand in hand. It brings a smile to my face, makes me giggle with glee (yeah, giggle), and warms my heart. That will be my Ryan and I someday—except, pretty sure I'll be riding piggyback, yelling yeehaw! And he will be happy to oblige.

After working long, ungodly amounts of hours as a manager at the company where we met, my Ryan moved on to bigger and better things. And before he knew it, nine years had flown by working as a field engineer tech for a worldwide phone company. This title and duties meant on his own, no one around, no walls closed in on him, a free-on-the road man. Ryan later found himself promoted to network operations manager for Iowa. We whooped and hollered and cheered with excitement over this new position. How proud we were that his hard work paid off. This new title meant an office job, downtown, rush-hour traffic, guys to lead with offices to check in on across his territory…dun, dun, dun. Anyone who knows my quiet, "also likes his space," "leave me the hell alone," "much road rage with a tiny bite" Ryan knew this new adventure should be very interesting. Meaning, "Lord help us all!" Thankfully, within a few years, the actual human contact was at a minimum. Most of his days were spent on the phone with his techs or on manager conference calls, which all could be easily done from his home office.

You see, sometimes we have to jump in and do something that's not really in our nature, as it always works out in the end and sometimes, just sometimes, leads to much bigger and better opportunities! Work hard, go with the flow, put your head down, and charge through it with a "you got this" attitude!

I'm Freaking Out

Your crazy is showing, you might
want to tuck that back in…
—Unknown

It all happened so fast; as if that dreaded checklist was in place. Two days after high school graduation, I packed up and moved to Ankeny, Iowa, which was like a city compared to my hometown of Ida Grove, Iowa. I had a full schedule of college classes and started a part-time job in the paint department at that local contract-supply store. Within a year, I found myself with a dainty ring on my finger. A year later, I had graduated from college and was hired as a (gasp) nine-to-five, "in an office" desktop publisher. And it was quickly followed by the big tulle, princess dress wedding ceremony, all in the same month. We soon were locked in with a mortgage, and then I felt a bit off at twenty-one years of age.

It took three months of feeling off before it hit me what I needed to do. I peed on that stick and the pink line proved my suspicions. I sat a bit in our little bathroom, stunned. I stood, anxious and in shock with my hand on the doorknob. I walked out in a daze and announced the news to my Ryan. Of course, we were ecstatic and couldn't wait to tell the world. Back then, kiddos, there was no social media. No one-time type out and post and the job is done. We actually had to pick up the phone—a landline. No cell phones back then either. How on earth did we function! We called long distance to my folks back home. Without skipping a beat, we jumped in the car to drive fifteen minutes over to my in-laws. We were gathered around the kitchen island, doing our usual "Hello, how was your day," with my mother-in-law being such a gracious host in offering the alcoholic beverages when my Ryan said, "No, Jenn can't drink that anymore." With a quick hands-on-the-hips scoff, she got adorably defensive. She was/is a size tiny and always done up to a T...so umm, yeah, "adorably."

"Who says she can't drink?"

My father-in-law caught on quickly and showed the big "Happy Chef" grin from ear to ear, all while my mother-in-law still stood disgusted with the refrigerator door open. Once all was caught up-to-date, it was a great shock, then excitement, and oh the plans that were set in motion from there on out.

During the pregnancy adventure, my Ryan laughed at my cravings. My unusual requests consisted of what he called a person's normal diet. I craved and devoured BK broilers like a champ. Normally, I had a clean diet. I never was much of a meat eater. Well, unless my hunter dad would bring me deer jerky. Then and only then would my carnivore side go full throttle. It would be ugly, and I would pay for it for weeks after.

I was so young, naïve, and unsettled. I never did get really big—just looked like a chubby girl with a large chest and buns to match. But to me, I felt like a beached whale and couldn't stand the feeling anymore. My clothes weren't fitting, and my Ryan's shirts weren't cutting it for me at seven and a half months, so he took me to the dreaded mall. Ugh, I so wasn't a girly girl then. The sales gal immediately grabbed a strap-on belly bump and said, "Put this on because you're going to get much bigger, sweetie." Me being tired, hormonal, and hungry teared up and got defensive immediately. Remember, I was already seven and a half whole months. I put in my time and felt I earned the respect that I was a full pregnant belly, dammit! So yeah, that poor sales gal didn't get any sales that trip and poor Ryan had to help emotional, "I'm so over this damn trip" me out of the store.

We were getting closer to the due date, and the nerves were setting in of what is to come—the unexpected. I think my experienced coworkers at times were sensing it and were trying to give support with their own stories. One had particularly scarred me: she was telling me what I would feel when the time comes and then what to do. I must have tuned most of it out in my loner kind of way. All I remember is her very loudly saying, "You push like you're taking a very large poop, just with an audience!" I'm pretty sure my eyes were huge, and I went blank from there. Okay now, stepping away. The fear of the whole scenario wasn't going over well with me. Obviously, all ended well due to my wise mother's advice: "Think the worst and concentrate on something else." That I did. I disconnected from what was going on at the time, and before I knew it, my baby boy, Ethan Douglas, was in my arms. Yes, I may have disconnected so much in my Collins' stubborn way and told Ryan I was so done and completely annoyed with the nurse screaming in my face; therefore, Ethan was vacuumed out and sported a nice cone-shaped head for a tad bit. Either way, he was in my arms and the job was done. Moving on.

Being in our early twenties and my Ryan working ungodly hours as a manager, still at the contract-supply store where we met, my mother came to stay with us for two weeks. Boy, was that appreciated. We had no idea what we were doing! The first night home we heard this screeching scream in the dead of the night. All three of us came running to his door in a panic—game on! We quickly learned, with confirmation from my three-time experienced mom, that this was not normal. During that first year, we heard that often. His first home day care provider told us, "This just isn't working for me." At that moment, I made the decision to quit my nine-to-five office job downtown, not to stay home with this new baby (remember, I still was getting the hang of this ride). I was shockingly hired on at a day care center. I could have my baby boy a few doors down from me—close enough to get to him, if he needed me or I needed my baby's cuddles, but enough space to do my own thing and learn how to even care for a child. When we had him in the day care center, a new teacher of his age group said, "Those babies need one teacher. That baby needs one teacher," not knowing that one baby she was pointing at was my baby boy. Oh, Ethan.

Ethan's lack of sleeping, fussiness, projectile vomiting, and colicky behavior had us deliriously sleep deprived. Therefore, of course we were in complete utter shock when I peed on that damn stick again to see a pink line so soon. Where's the brakes? Slam on the brakes!

I have to admit, I cried on the back steps after that discovery. Remember, I was tired, I was young, and our journey seemed like we were a Mac truck with the gas pedal stuck at full speed. When we brought home our Evan Dennis, Ethan, at two years of age, was still not sleeping through the night. He threw up most of what he ate, was still colicky, was constantly talking, and was a busy, busy boy. It came as a great surprise the first night home with our new little boy that he hadn't made a peep since putting him down. We were up with Ethan and in a panic rushed in to check on our Evan. Why wasn't he crying or hungry or needing us? The child was completely accommodating from day one. He would just chill and watch the Ethan show. Still does, to this day.

Sadly, the year the quiet little one was born, there were many cases of sudden infant death syndrome (SIDS). It was a great debate if babies should sleep on their stomachs, backs, sides, at an angle, or on their heads (kidding). Everyone had an opinion, experience, and suggestions. It had our heads spinning on what we should do. From the time Evan came along for this journey, he slept through the night about every night. He didn't make a peep; therefore, he concerned us even more. I mean, from our experience, babies were loud, fussy, and demanded our attention 24-7. We decided the best thing to assure us all is just fine is to have Evan sleep in a car seat next to our bed for his first year of life. This way we could reach over and check on him throughout the night.

By this time, I felt I was considered an experienced mama. I mean really, Ethan was like having four babies (remember, it was confirmed by another), so we felt comfortable enough for me to stay home with my boys for a few years before the workforce called me back.

My boys were adorable pacifier babies. Ethan loved his pacifiers, and we learned quickly it was a lifesaver with his crying. We almost forced it on Evan just because it was such an adorable look, but he really didn't get into it like his brother. Ethan was three years old when we tried to get serious about eliminating his pacifier habit. It was a hard habit to break—pretty sure a good comparison to caffeine, nicotine, or more likely a hard-core cocaine addiction. We cut the tips, put vinegar on the nipples, and even just threw his away. But that clever daredevil was notorious for shimmying up Evan's crib to crawl in and confiscate his brother's discarded pacifiers. Evan would just go with the flow and allow such Ethan shenanigans! In time we broke the habit, and Evan soon waved bye-bye to his own pacy without a fight. Again, he was so accommodating and chill, which was greatly appreciated!

I've learned now that there are all stages and phases of life. Much like a road trip; it's fun, it's exciting, it's scary, it's boring, it's sticky, it's tiring, and it's frustrating. It may not be going as planned, with speed bumps, frequent stops, detours, and total route changes, but it's still a great ride!

Sports? Didn't See That Coming

Safety first!

—Unknown

Marrying into the Timm family, it was quickly realized that sports was a given. Yeah, keep laughing. This "march to my own beat" chick and loner can ride with this one too. In the beginning, I was positive my Ryan was whispering in my ear, "Go, Vikings" in my sleep. Remember, he was from Minnesota and was a true, loyal fan. Even during their ugliest years, he wore the purple proud, even in public. Most family gatherings with this clan consisted of Viking attire and the game on. All the men gathered around the big screen, screaming out their approvals or disapprovals.

From the start with our boys, we had footballs, soccer balls, and tennis balls. Balls, balls, and more balls were always flying through the air and laying around the house. A basketball hoop was attached to our oak railing in our one and a half story great room, and the furniture was moved out regularly for large and small Timm men to play.

We even had the carpet replaced with laminate to make the game more successful. The kids' friends thought I was a cool mom and wife when in reality, I learned to pick my battles as a survival method!

Ryan signed both the boys up for sports as soon as it was available for their age. The first team sport both boys did was the local "Bam Bam." This was an introduction into baseball. A large rubber ball placed on top of two tin coffee cans that were duct tape together—hilarious! It was total chaos with three- and four-year-olds running the wrong way, doing the potty dance, and playing in the dirt. All had to take turns; there was no score keeping. Yeah, right. Those Timm men were keeping track in their heads.

My Ethan was bored as can be with this kiddie game. He let us know with every power hit, run, and glare from the base that he was forced to stop at instead of stealing the next base. From a very young age, he caught on to the concept of playing sports, and this standing around business, waiting for others to grasp the concept of running the correct direction, or the kids playing in the dirt instead of putting the ball back on the duct tape coffee cans for the next batter annoyed him terribly. Bam Bam was short-lived for him, and we moved him into T-ball as soon as the age limit allowed. Now our Evan, on the other hand, took this new activity as seriously and politely as humanly possible. He paid close attention to every detail told by his coach and sat patiently far away from the other kids to avoid getting dirty or pushed in the chaos. He hit the ball with proper force and ran to the base to be given the next instruction from the base coach—all with serious determination. Both boys made us laugh and smile with pride as the whole local Timm clan and our friends stood on the sidelines. They were the boys' own personal cheering squad. The fever of sports had been felt, so now it had begun. Both boys were signed up for basketball, soccer, golf, baseball, and tackle football. Yes, both. It really wasn't a choice; they must stay active and try it all. Ryan coached a majority of these sports, and I stood as the proud mama (I was their JennJenn) on the sidelines in my color coordinating T-shirt and dangling earrings (I left the heels at home...sometimes).

Around ten years of age, we realized this sporty thing just wasn't for Evan. He had the talent; he just didn't have the passion that Ethan had for it. He firmly told us, "Just because I like baseball doesn't mean I need to play it all the time." We got his quiet message. It became very clear Evan's passion lay elsewhere. Ethan, on the other hand, breathed, ate, and slept sports. We even have photos of him sleeping with trophies. He studied college and pro stats, most likely the only thing he did ever read through his school days. Sorry, teachers, he never did read those English assignments. He and Ryan stayed up late watching Monday night football and talking the night away about plays, stats, and players. Of course, I tried to be interested during these television games, but it was clear I was annoying the hell out of my guys trying to keep up. I tried, I really did. But I didn't get what all the hype was about. Well, until Jared Allen came on board with the Vikings—awe, wiping away my drool. Then, and only then, the game became interesting. His Fathead replica almost got applied next to my bed, not the game room wall as planned. I quickly lost interest, once again, when he left the team.

Ethan was not only on the regular teams, but he also had been asked to play on tournament teams. Ryan was requested to coach these boys on many occasions. It was great; we met a lot of good families, and we grew close to them while warming the hard bleachers together. Those were the days you practiced three, four times a week and played tournament baseball or football from Friday night to Sunday night. We enjoyed many memorable hours together with these families. I will always cherish those years. Even if we don't see some of the families anymore, they were very good memories, with several late nights in a garage replaying the days game with some cold drinks, all while the kiddos played the sport again in the backyard. Good times!

We knew baseball season was upon us when the privacy protective cups started appearing around the house like it was part of our home decor. It was baseball life, just how it was. Only once did I find this season ritual a bit disturbing. Ethan had just walked in from an hour and a half, hot, sweaty practice. Talking a mile a minute, he reached in, pulled out, and laid *it* on my beautiful, custom, and really "just for looks" dining room table. He continued up the stairs to take his long-awaited shower when the little one came bouncing in, noticed the cup on the table, and put it up to his face to say, "Luke, I am your father." Without skipping a beat, he put it down in its original placement and continued on his way, all while I stood there in complete shock from the first scene of pulling it out and the placement. Yep, we didn't eat much at that table during those years; it was more of a gathering ground for an assortment of things, obviously. That table was disinfected on a regular basis.

These were the years our Ethan earned his name Big-E. He was always a bit smaller than his peers. Lean, due to his gluten-free diet. A life hiccup confirmed around seven years of age when he was finally and correctly diagnosed with celiac sprue disease. Those beginning years all make sense now! (Possibly a whole other book warming up. We'll see. Wink, wink.)

Around junior high, Ethan gave up basketball and was focusing on baseball and football. Then out of nowhere, wrestling was introduced to this boy. Oh, how I loved wrestling. I say this very dramatically. Try it again: Oh, how I loved wrestling! The extreme focus, one-on-one, intense, "moment on the mat" sport. It could also have been my favorite due to the indoor-climate controlled environment. His first moment on the mat resulted in a victory pin in twenty-three seconds, second pin in second period, third pin in fifty-two seconds—that's my Ethan, and I was instantly hooked as his number one fan! I thoroughly loved those sweaty, huge-grin, heart-pumping hugs after a match. I craved them and still giggle from the memory of them.

The staleness, the sweaty boys, the hard, crammed-together bleachers, the stench in the air weekend after weekend; but the entertainment of my Ethan whooping butt on the mat and watching my tiny mother-in-law getting aggressive on the bleachers in her pencil skirt and stilettos, grabbing anyone around her with her acrylic nails, shaking them and then kneeing the elderly man in front of her, all while screaming step-by-step instructions made it all worth it! Oh yes, all had to watch out for Ethan and his adorable, proud grandma during those days!

We once found ourselves in a crunch time in the Timm home to cut weight before a fast approaching Saturday tournament. Ryan committed to riding his bike all over town while Ethan ran. All food in the refrigerator had been replaced with veggies and fruits. Protein shakes were being mixed up, and the youngest one was throwing a complete fit that he, too, was going to starve. Apparently, at the time, we all were cutting weight. This boy was determined, and we were going to be his cheerleaders all the way. Go, Ethan, go! This was a total family commitment at this point because we had a match to attend!

Before we knew it, the second year of wrestling was upon us with a sixteen-man bracket, and guess who qualified for state, baby! What a thrill. It was so intense. Yes, I got the proud mama team shirt. I was exhausted watching, screaming and controlling my actions at those matches. Who knew sports could be so much fun, exhilarating, and draining!

He, we, everyone bounced from football to wrestling to baseball. The seasons blended together, and when one sadly ended, we were fired up for the next showdown. Who would have thought this chick would be caught up in such craziness and loving every minute of it. I still had no idea what was going on, but the look on my boys' face made up for my lack of sport knowledge. The excitement and gained friendships in the stands, the thrill of the sidelines, the anticipation of how it all turns out, the exhaustion of the day, and the laughs when replaying the day that evening. Funny, I don't remember attending one sporting event in my own teen years. I remember my brother (four years older) was a wrestler. For a person always game to try new things, how on earth did I miss out on watching this sport all those years? My sister (fourteen months younger) was in sports. But I don't remember getting caught up in the excitement and thrill. I guess I should have attended at least one game to see; I was just too busy cruising doing my own thing.

With all the excitement, running, and games, the years flew by with trophies and medals piling up. Just like that, we were on to the high school years.

Are you ready for some football! Freshman year with his first tackle of the season, fierce and awesome and...then as quickly as it started, we were watching from the sidelines for six weeks. Yep, you guessed it—a break. Our first break for this rambunctious, highly active child was in the thumb! A thumb. A stupid thumb swelled up the whole hand for days. It broke across the growth plate on the right hand, his writing hand. We were told to take this break serious; to heal properly for his adult years. He must cast it, not use it, baby it—yeah, yeah, yeah. My heart sank. I was set on the thrill of the season—to watch my boy's expressions and body language on the field. At this point I was fully committed to sports. I still didn't get the rules, but that was never my style. Ryan looked like he was going to vomit, but we composed ourselves for Ethan. I have to admit, it was hard to fake, as the tears were on the verge of exploding, knowing my boy couldn't join his team and run with a ball for six weeks! Ethan was so bummed and a bit miffed we took him to the doctor in the first place.

As an experienced mom of Ethan, I firmly stated the cast needed to be black to hide dirt, food, and God knows whatever else this teenage boy would get all over it. Within days, it was chewed on, wrapping was coming out from within, and it smelled horrendous! Scented room sprays weren't helping it. Body sprays weren't helping it. Then our Jake (my brother's well-deserved nickname for Ethan at the time; Jake from *Two and a Half Men*, if you have watched the show, you get it) jumped into a pool! He said he fell in getting a ball for his buddies who were in the pool. So yeah, he jumped in, yelling, "Yeehaw!" And we all know it. He was caught up in the moment. He's so my son.

An extremely long six weeks later at the follow-up appointment, Ethan had two choices at the doctor's office:

1. No more cast, wear a splint for two weeks, but still no football.
2. Put on another thicker cast for three weeks that covers his thumb, past his wrist, and be free to play football.

Guess which one he chose? Yes! Good choice, my boy. JennJenn was back, ready for action with her padded stadium chair. Sorry, it's just not as thrilling of a game unless your boy is out there. Oh yeah, and Ethan got to finish out the season with his buddies and use the club as a good blocker. And just like that, the football season ended.

The gorging on gluten-free pasta, ice cream, and popcorn after a game came to an end as well. The little one noticing announced, "Boy, Ethan, you have really let yourself go!" Yikes, it's going to get dramatic in the Timm house once again as wrestling season and cutting weight is fast approaching. Let the next round begin!

As quickly as his high school career started for football and wrestling, it ended when a bad concussion kept him home from school for a couple of weeks. We decided, as much as we loved the sports and watching him play those two sports, our job was to raise a functioning adult, and we knew big college scholarships and a further career wasn't necessarily part of his ride. Although at the time, we let him keep his sport of choice: baseball. It, too, quickly ended his first month in college with a torn labrum in his shoulder. Two surgeries later, almost six months of healing…sigh, the white flag is up. We get it; the sport ride has officially ended!

Many may ask, "All those years running, all those checks written for clubs, hotels, fees, and equipment, in the end, was it worth it given the outcome?" Hell *yes*, it was! I believe the discipline of the sports, the support of his team, and the mentoring of his coaches helped mold this young man. I can't say thank you enough for such great entertainment we got out of this sporting experience. The friendships that were formed, hours of excitement, and the many memories that we will cherish outweighs it all. Besides, what else would we have done with those years? It still was time, money, and energy well spent.

Ethan Douglas, we are so proud of the strong, responsible, hardworking young man he has turned into. From the way he handles his celiac disease with grace and the 100 percent he gave to his sports and the attempt for help with his studies that didn't come easily for him. He brought humor to our house with his Jake moments and teasing. Life is a party to Big-E, and he could find the good and fun in about any situation. He once told me, "They did a bad thing, Mom. It doesn't make them a bad person." We love our Ethan and can always count on him to do a job well done with full commitment and a hilarious replay story to follow up.

It's a Hip-Hop World

Go big or go home.
                    —Unknown

Our "one blue eye and one brown eye" Mr. Evan started out on his life journey with barely a peep. He's always been interesting with his early year Mohawks, then an ongoing hat fetish, and intriguing attire choices. At a very young age, he was told by a salesclerk in a store, "You have your own style, little dude." He brings smiles to our faces with his quick wit and many character personalities. He had a peculiar way of walking by railings, grabbing them and pulling himself horizontal in the air, or jumping on a table to body twerk, then politely sit down again without an explanation. He makes us stop and see this world in a new view—a more chillaxed way. Later, as a teenager, his response to about anything was, "Mkah"(okay), which could bring my Ryan to a boil in a second or at times, it seemed fitting as he used it. He was a mystery to his teachers. "I don't have him figured out yet" was honestly repeated at second semester school conferences more than once. To watch a quiet, reserved child find his passion on stage, with a spotlight, in the world of dance had us all stunned!

Around age five, our sweet little Evan came to us wanting to learn to dance like the guy he was watching on a music video on television. We were quite surprised by this request since Evan was quiet, reserved, and serious minded, but we were going to do whatever we could to fulfill this request because the child never asked for anything. We found a local dance studio and put him in a few classes, one with all boys and one with boys and girls. He seemed to enjoy it, although you would never have known since he wasn't ever that overly expressive child. Remember, that was last chapter, our Big-E.

After five years at this dance studio, performing only onstage once a year at recital time, he seemed to grow bored and anxious to take it to the next level. We are forever thankful to have been directed to check out another studio known for their hip-hop choreography among the dance community in our area. His goal was to take his dance passion to the next level, and boy did he!

The first month at this new hip-hop studio, trying out for the competition team, he was placed in with the advanced teen groups. During his audition, one coach took his own shoes off to toss them, and one coach threw his hat. In the comedian world, this means you suck. But apparently, in the hip-hop world, when one gets items tossed at them, this is good, sick, killer. This quiet, reserved, and tiny child surprised them and nailed the audition with such confidence. They were left shocked while Evan strolled out of the room in complete Evan composure. And that moment confirmed more nights and weekends away from the home. What a fun, crazy, expensive, new world just opened up to us!

Our calendar was full. It was colorful, and we all were high-fiving one another as we passed through the garage door. I'm not going to brag, just confidently say my boys rock and kept us entertained in two different worlds. Ryan and I found ourselves once more caught up in the excitement and thrill of this experience. As all parents should feel this—be their cheerleaders, folks, and they will be yours!

Evan was in his sixth year of dancing and now first year at competition level. He had been working hard all that first year at the new studio—hour after hour, night after night at practices, weekend after weekend at workshops and competitions. He was putting in 100 percent, sweating his little buns off, all to be ready for recital and then off to nationals in another state for the final season competition. Typical, the first call to me at work the morning of recital was a scratchy voice, coughing Evan saying he was going to throw up. Ugh, what timing! He made it through the day with plenty of rest, fluids, and on to the original showtime with style, yet why wouldn't our Evan? He's *always* full of surprises, and the show must go on!

After a year at this new studio, he realized, in order to take this interest further, he needed to explore all forms of dance. Okay, fine, he may have come to this realization after several choreographers told him. Therefore, lyrical, tap, and jazz were added to his schedule, along with his hip-hop. Cha-ching, cha-ching, cha-ching. He was determined and passionate and by all means, his father and I were going to do everything possible for him to further his interest, dream, and given talent. He was promised lyrical was added just as a class to learn and practice the skills. But before he knew it, he was worked into a lyrical competition routine, leaving a few parents teared up and in awe. It was confirmed he had a natural form and just knew what to do with his poses without being coached.

I may be biased here, but our boy was *amazing*! We know this because we heard it many times over by adults, the studio directors, and other dancers. He wowed many and brought tears to a few. He drew attention from other studios and choreographers. He received whispering in his ear "Money" a few times by our studio director as she rubbed her fingers together and winked at him. It also was confirmed by his distant uncle who was visiting from out of state (Ryan's oldest brother), as he causally lounged out in the audience, ready for his nephew to take the stage. And after five seconds of the performance, he looked over to us in a shocked, "what the hell is this" dramatic "Whhhaaaat!" We once saw one rather blessed-sized male judge in his purple satin button-down and black leather pants jump to his feet and give him a standing ovation after his solo, all while another mom said to us, "They don't normally do that." We knew our boy had it going on then. Someone so little became a giant on that stage. We were all so stunned, proud, giggling, and in awe.

It was fun to watch my Ryan during these years as well. This diehard sports-minded man's competitive side came out, and he was heavily involved in Evan's audition pieces and practices. Ryan seemed so competitive I thought he was going to jump on stage a few times with excitement. Like at a sporting event, he couldn't sit back and watch. He needed to get involved, so he found his spot behind the scenes for a couple seasons, helping the props make their way to the stage with many other just as excited and proud fathers. He did get his time on stage when a parent dance was put together. You see, when you write enough checks, you also get your time on stage to shine! Yes, Ryan was front and center, giving it his all with jazz hands and hip wiggling. We both had a blast and could feel the excitement of having the spotlight on us for a change.

The greatest oak was once a little nut who held his own.
—Unknown

Around this time of switching studios and taking it to the next level, it came to my attention that my hip-hopper was getting called names those middle school years because he was a dancer. At the time, the boy had danced for the past six years, was twelve years old, and was going into seventh grade when the labeling started in. Middle school years are the worse, and this Mama Bear had no tolerance when it came to attacking my cubs. We talked, talked, and talked to our boys about nay-sayers and to ignore, laugh it off, look the other way, and stand up for yourselves—to just be you. These peeps are just spouting off or jealous because they haven't found their passion or have the support of family and friends behind them. How terribly sad! In true Evan fashion, he handled it all very well. Trust me, if I had heard or seen it happen directly, I would have gone ape shit on the kid like the mother in the movie *This Is 40* (a must-watch for parents without kids around)! With that being said, any of us with children all know as soon as we open our mouths to point something out on others, we are accommodated with the oh so pleasant feeling of hearing our own child has, in turn, called someone a name. So with that said, my Timm men and myself included are guilty of such behavior, and shame on us as well. Imperfect human beings we all are. Therefore, we must develop a thick skin and brush it off and move on.

Back to Evan. He had one kid (we didn't know his last name or parents to handle ourselves) picking on him constantly anytime he saw him. Evan's friends would try to defend him; the bully just shoved the friends and kept at Evan. So our sweet, reserved, quiet Evan jacked the jackass in the face! (Yep, here I go already, name-calling.) We don't condone hitting, but he did try to handle it in the steps we laid out for him and felt he was against a wall. The kid just wouldn't stop. But guess what? That kid left him alone from that day forward. Evan confirms it by saying, "Yep, I'm a badass" with a wink. Love his spirit! And honestly, Evan never seemed to get worked up. He seemed to always have the "whatever" attitude. We all need a bit more of that! Soon after, many learned of his talent, his gained reputation, and awards, so that phase died off as quickly as it started. Just a phase. A silly, silly middle-school phase.

Life changed bluntly for us as Evan ended his tenth year of dancing and fifth year competing with many hours, nights, weekends, and full weeks away from his squad when he suddenly, quietly, and firmly decided to turn in his dancing shoes and passion, with sad regrets from many. There was no further discussion about it. He stated it and didn't want to talk about it anymore, period, and reminded us it was his decision. He was in to his early high school years, and his squad needed him at the skate park. In time I got it. I was once there too. All we can say is, those many hours in the studio, working on balance and a strong core, made a kick ass skateboarder out of him. So win-win either way.

Many gave Evan hugs, cheers, and screams of support through the years. We truly appreciated it! It takes all of us as a community to raise our children proud, strong, and on the right path for a successful human. Be there for each other. Find your support group to raise your children strong, adventurous, and brave. To all of you and your children: pursue your interest, find the courage to live your dream, shine proud, and by all means let your girls play football and your boys dance, if they so desire to!

Evan Dennis, our adorable, sweet, creative, quick-witted, honest (too honest), eccentric Mr. Evan. The boy who excels in all that he tries. This is a child who teaches himself a whole song on an electric guitar in one evening. He keeps us in suspense for his next move. He has us shaking our heads and on a complete adventure! Our boy reminds us daily to not take life so seriously. Everything doesn't need to be turned into a competition. Life doesn't need to be a big show. To sit back, chill, and enjoy. All we ask of you, Evan, is to just be happy. Go ahead, be a peacock, and fly, *mkah*!

The Zoo

I'm suspicious of people who don't like dogs.
But I trust a dog when it doesn't like a person.
—Billy Murray

Pets have been a very important part of our journey. I grew up with pets in and outside of the home and knew I would always have them as part of my family. When we moved to our third home, Ryan brought home a cat from the local animal shelter. Cats, he informed me, were low maintenance yet were snugglers. He grew up around indoor cats. I, of course, growing up on acreage, had outdoor cats. This uncomfortableness of having this creature in the home found me outside, waiting while the kitten explored the home and Ryan was off getting all the appropriate supplies. That feeling quickly passed, and I felt our Happy cat (yes, of course I let the three-year-old, at the time, name the cat Happy) needed a buddy, so Tiger joined us soon after, a.k.a. Crabby Cat, as later named by nephew Dylan (Ryan's younger sister's oldest son).

A short two years later, we bought a new house in a neighboring development. We found ourselves welcoming Marley to our home—an adorable purebred basset hound.

We had this pathetic-looking, drooling, dumb puppy for less than a year, and boy, oh boy were the cats pissed the entire time. Sadly, we lost our Marley before Easter—the month of his one-year birthday, exactly two weeks after fencing in our backyard just for him. It was due to an unusual *sock* diet. The dog was flipping amazing, confirmed by his vet too. Apparently, carpet, cell phones, remotes, and drywall were tasty, along with his preference of socks. It was not unusual to see the boys tackled to the ground and their socks eaten off them within seconds. After the winter snow melted, we saw the evidence of the amount of such diet. The entire backyard was full of socks, wash cloths, and a number of other items that had successfully passed through. I'm convinced the saying "The dog ate my homework" originated from the basset hound snacking.

It was extremely hard on us; therefore, soon after Eddie, a.k.a. Eduardo the boxer, joined the family and what a joy he was! We're sleeping through the night, enjoying our new cozy socks, and can actually have our belongings out without fear of being swallowed up. The cats continued to be miffed with us during those days. We aimed to continue our pattern of totally pissing them off.

Ed from day one had been the most obedient, well-behaved, beloved dog ever. For a boxer, we had been blessed. He was an oversized boxer and beautifully described as big-boned, solid, or "one magnificent beautiful beast." He was weighing in at his top winter weight of one hundred and twenty pounds. Yep, he was a full-bred boxer. He was not overweight, just beautifully blessed in size. We reminded people to stop staring; it makes him self-conscious! Ed was my bed-spooning furnace. We all loved him! He was a favorite to all who knew him. Even my grandmother requested a Christmas photo with him to send out to all she knew. They sat side by side together, her in a Christmas hat and him with a matching scarf. It was a great family memory how she had a framed picture of Ed in her bedroom.

Some of my children have four legs and
leave hair wherever they go...
—*Unknown*

Now around Ed's fifth birthday, we started to see him aging, maybe getting a bit lazy. After much consultation with others who knew our Ed, we all decided he was depressed. Yep, dogs can get that way too. Therefore, we took the advice to get him a buddy. Welcome OLIVER! A full-bred pug. OLIVER! was always in all caps with an explanation point during the beginning years. Then, later for a short time, renamed to Sir-Shits-Alot. Once again, the cats were pissed off! OLIVER! was something else. He has been my little snuggler from day one, and I was told on more than one occasion to stop carrying him like a baby. I thought Ed was going to snort him up being so tiny! A pug was "the assholes of all breeds," according to my older brother. But I adored him, and so did our Ed. He was his protector and took it as his duty to watch over his new little buddy like an older brother. It was a beautiful friendship from the start.

After several years of having our cats in our home, I started making subtle hints that they should be moved to the garage. They preferred to be outside 85 percent of the time anyway. Life changes, hiccups happen, and unfortunately the cats were caught up in the cause. Our Ethan's most recent breathing issues was the perfect push to go full force with the plan. I was on a cleaning spree, ridding my house of the cats. Everywhere I went, they had a mess of either hair clumps, vomit, their food tossed down our vents, litter all over the storage room, hair, hair, and their litter box leaked on an area rug. Did I mention hair? And I was forever chasing dogs away from eating their dumps. After several hours of cleaning and purging out rooms, they had a nice setup in our three-car garage, complete with several bed options, food, and litter box. The next part of this cat purging party: the appropriate cleaning companies came out to do a pet elimination carpet clean, dryer vent clean, and duct clean. So my mom and sister would also be safe to stay while in my home without their eyes swelling up, watering, and itching to the point of the appearance of pink eye. Eventually, we relocated the cats from our home. Sadly, with our busy schedules, it took almost two weeks before one of the boys even questioned their absence. I don't think the dogs ever did notice their exit.

In April 2014, we found ourselves terribly heartbroken. With family and friends who were diagnosed with cancer, loss of other pets, and living with a celiac, we were no strangers to bad, disturbing, and sad news. We deal with it and move on; it is what it is. With tears streaming down our faces and the news given to our beyond heartbroken boys, we felt this one had sucker punched us and felt like our hearts were ripped out. We had to get our family photos taken and say our goodbyes as we had to put our beloved buddy, pal, and our love Ed to sleep on April 25, 2014. He was seven years old. He had started to sleep the majority of his days and couldn't use his hind legs. Several trips to the local vet then on to a veterinary hospital confirmed that a lump was found in his stomach and a mass in his spine. If he survived the first surgery, they had no idea if they could attempt the second. Taking in account of his age, the breed, and the situation, we all made the decision together. All four of us were sobbing, telling him we loved him and held him to the end. We were reassured the night before while doing our family photos that he agreed with the decision, too, when he sat up front and center during one of the pictures with a huge grin. He hadn't sat up in days, so he told us it's going to be okay, and it's time.

We're blessed to have had him. We smile at the memories, and we still tear up that we couldn't keep him with us forever.

In time, with wonderful, supportive, and kind words from friends and family, we found ourselves smiling from favorite Ed stories brought up. Smiling about the abundance of dog food that OLIVER! will take a year to get through, although it would have taken Ed a week. Smiling how clean our floors were without the puddles of drinking water from Ed shoving his entire face in the bowl. Smiling at the memories of Ed and one of our friends sharing Funyun chips mouth-to-mouth on more than one camping occasions. Smiling over how awesome and helpful the Timm boys were with Ryan away in Georgia for work the following week, as they were scared to make me cry more.

Smiling about how fresh the house was without Ed's ham-bone gas. Smiling over the super cool earrings I got from a coworker—how awkward I made them all feel with my bloodshot, swollen eyes all of the last week. Smiling over how empty our bedroom was without Ed's twin-size mattress, comforter, and pillow. Smiling at the beautiful flowers sent from a dear friend. Smiling at the backyard landmines and the found Ed hair on our clothing that I would leave for a while longer. And of course, smiling about all the hugs, kind words, and poems from anyone and everyone who knew us. We felt truly blessed during such a difficult time. This loss felt like a child was ripped from our family and continues to hurt today. We now celebrate every year with an addition to his weeping willow in our backyard, where his ashes were laid to rest. Our hearts go out to everyone who has ever lost a human child, because this feeling was truly awful. I couldn't imagine your heartbreak.

The heartache not only affected us humans, but our Oliver took on a new "lost soul" behavior. He was clearly confused and became very attached to us. He was my little buddy, and I continued to carry him around like a baby everywhere because at this point, we helped each other move on.

At that time, Oliver was going to doggy day care during the days to keep him social and distracted. On a Friday afternoon, Ryan and I went the usual time to pick him up and got talking with the owner, a dear friend. A yellow Lab caught our attention. We learned this dog had been left there due to her owner battling cancer, and no one in the family was available to help with the Lab. This poor Lab was stuck at the doggy day care for eight months, and you could tell she was itching to get outside to run. We felt a push to offer to bring her home for the weekend to let her run. The day care owner agreed she needed it. Five years later, we still have our beautiful, stubborn Ms. MirMar. She makes it perfectly clear she is not here to play with the needy pug, but it's her duty to roam outside as she pleases.

Two years later, I started following a pug rescue site on social media. I was drawn to the pugs and their snorting, snoring, lazy, loving nature. Then old man Jeff appeared on my social media feed, and I just had to have him! Jeff was a ten-year-old puppy mill dump. He "wasn't in to the ladies anymore" is all we were told from the rescue group. He was half blind, half deaf, and had hip dysplasia. When we first got him, he could barely run without dragging his hind legs. He couldn't walk up steps, wasn't comfortable being held, was clearly never on furniture, had no idea what to do with a toy, and just sat on the floor, staring at all of us, ghostly. Fast forward six months after constant love, attention, daily walks, medication for his hips, healthy food, and snuggles on the couch, he is now running around the house, dragging toys out, playing with Oliver, and acting like a ten-month-old puppy. Old man Jeff is the best, and I can't believe some heartless person had this dog in a wire cage for ten whole years and didn't show him an ounce of love.

It wasn't even a year later from Jeff's welcome to the family when a huge flubber doll of a pug showed up on my social media feed. Without skipping a beat, Ryan and I were on our way to Kansas City to pick up Hugo. Oh,

Hugo, what can we say. He is the absolute laziest dog we have ever had. He leans his head on a table, leans against a wall, lays on his back with his legs spread on every surface that he can and halfway through a walk. Let's just say he has tea bagged Ryan a time or two with his neck sag as well. Hugo had an instant bromance with Oliver; they are not shy about their awkward licking, buddy obsession, and snuggling. Eight-year-old Hugo molded into the family as if he was always with us. We are now complete with a full grumble. We feel he is half Shar-Pei and half pug—a big boy of hanging skin. As if he had lost a hundred pounds and has to carry around the sagging past. He is absolutely glorious and adored, man boobs and all!

There are so many furbabies needing our help. If we all do our part and share our loving homes, what an amazing experience you will have as an entire family. I cannot stress this enough. Do your research when buying a pure-bred puppy. Know where the parents are kept. Ask about the parents. Make sure they aren't just breeding machines. Check out any rescue in your state and hear the stories they have seen; it's heartbreaking. Adopt, don't shop. It is a very rewarding experience: the love and appreciation they show toward you. You will have a buddy for life!

Road Trips with the Timms

Let the good times roll.

—Unknown

I shake my head that I'm even repeating this. We got the sad news that a family friend had passed away. So my Timm clan traveled for the funeral. It was a very nice service. And as expected, it was an extremely heartbreaking service. Of course, these kinds of moments get you thinking, and since we had a few hours' trip back home, I asked what I thought was a very serious question. Which I should have known, at that time of seventeen years with my man, was a *stupid* question. "Would you like to be buried or cremated?" First response obviously was, "I don't care, I'm dead." Me, not giving up so quickly, "No, really, what would you like done?" Then I get this, as serious as he can be: "I want to be stuffed with one leg propped up on a barrel and a drink in my hand." In honor of his preferred adult drink: Captain Morgan. I love my Ryan and can honestly say I would be terribly lost without him. But there is no way in hell I'm keeping him stuffed in my house, so let's get the plan in place now. Who's taking stuffed, "knee propped up," "drink in his hand" Ryan? At this point, I had given up on the conversation, so I sat and enjoyed the view out my window. Then we heard as serious, curious, and dry as can be from the little one in the back seat: "So who found him [the family friend] and how do we know that person didn't do something to him?" Awkward silence…a bit inner panic, and a subtle glance from the corners of our eyes to each other. Ryan and I sat a bit stunned, pondering how to respond to this odd and very twisted thought coming from our ten-year-old. Obviously, we watched a bit too much crime scene shows on television. Thankfully, the rest of the trip went on quietly with everyone listening to the radio, and we made it home without any incidences, blow ups, or spills.

I wear hearing aids in both ears. I struggle to hear full conversations, especially in a vehicle with background noise. But I usually hear enough of a conversation or sentence to piece together what's going on. So we're on yet another trip, driving along with the boys, and Ethan's talking away (shocker). He usually isn't even talking to anyone in particular. He just talks. When I hear "And his nipples were larger than my head!" Giggle, giggle…and back to zoning out, minding my own business, and taking in the scenery I go. In these cases, I don't ask for a repeat of what else he said because, really, do I want to know who, what, why on this one? Yikes! Yes, it's moments like this I'm glad for my hearing loss!

Leading up to the day of a trip can be very eventful with the Timm boys, as we once found ourselves on packing day for our trip to the in-law's Arizona home. The boys were in their early teen years, and a trip away from our busy schedule is just what we all needed. It took our Evan all of two minutes to do the packing task. After inspection of his suitcase, Ryan states, "Evan, we're going for seven days. There are only three socks [not pairs] and random shorts in here." Evan states, as casual as can be with a shrug, "It's vacation, not like I'm going to shower, change, or wear a shirt." True. Good point, son. Way to keep it simple. Although, no underwear? (Raise of eyebrows.) We should just be happy he had shorts packed. I guess we were going to Arizona to swim and relax in the hot sun; swimming trunks don't require undergarments. This child had life figured out from a very young age. Keep it simple, don't complicate things, avoid a checked bag at the airport. Don't overdo and just enjoy the moment!

When the boys entered their seventh and freshman grade year of school, I planned a mini road trip up north to check on my nephew, Tyler, at college (my brother's oldest child). Ethan, who was fourteen years old with his learners and school permit, was quite the skilled driver. Therefore, I took full advantage of this excellent opportunity. Yes! Finally, I have a chauffeur, folks! We found the college with no problems. He swung into the parking spot with ease. Tyler greeted us and showed us dorm living. We met his roommates, received a mini tour of the campus, took him out to eat, stocked him up on food, and bought him a blender. Really, doesn't every college student need a blender for their protein shakes? Seriously, people, what were you thinking the blender was for? On the way home, I thanked the boys for such an enjoyable day and asked what they got out of the experience. Ethan, with complete enthusiasm, said, "So let me get this straight, in college you get to live with your buddies and hang out all day? *Awesome!*" Evan, curious as can be, asked, "Why would they make their beds?" I'm laughing at their two completely different assessments of the trip. That whole day, after everything we saw, that's what they got out of the day? But stopping to really think about it, yeah, those were the days, and how cool it was to live with your friends, to just hang out, laugh, and be there with one another? And why were their beds made? Did they do that for us? Did I make my bed in college? Thinking…thinking. Dang, I can't remember yesterday. How can I remember waaaay back then? Awe, such good college boys. Your mamas should be proud. Obviously, Evan has absolutely no plans of ever making his bed again after he's moved out and doesn't have me nagging to do it. I tried. As for Ethan, he has no time to make a bed. He's got plans out with his buddies!

So yeah, plan many road trips in your life. They can be awkward, relaxing, exciting, fun, and weird. Keep it simple, enjoy life, and just don't question the large nipples! Any takers yet for stuffed Ryan?

Organized Chaos

Remember, as far as anyone knows,
we're a normal family…
—Homer Simpson

From a very young age, we taught our boys to do chores. Whether it was putting away clothes, picking up toys, folding laundry, or simply clearing the dishes from the dinner table, they had daily chores. Whatever was needed to be completed around the house, they were taught to pitch in and help. I grew up with chores. My kids were going to have the same responsibility. I was given the task to raise boys, and I was going to raise these boys to be good partners someday—to help around their own homes just like their father does. We all took part in keeping this house running. Ryan and I both worked outside the home at this time. We all lived in the home. We were all taking part in cleaning the home. It was never a big deal. It was pretty simple. You wanted money from us to go do something, you worked a bit around the house. You want to go out with your buddies at night or on the weekend, you worked around the house first. Remember, work hard, play hard.

We got to the point when the boys were too young for jobs outside the home but old enough to do more activities or fun that required money. We came up with a deal. For every dollar we spend, you owe us a chore. It worked pretty darn smoothly for a number of years until the mid-teenage years when the toys and outings were a bit more expensive. Thankfully, by then they had their own jobs, and we came up with a new deal of matching fifty-fifty toward the requests.

Now keep in mind, we didn't let those boys half-ass their chores so they could rush out and meet their pals. I had a certain way laundry was to be folded, and if it wasn't done right, I made them refold. Do the job correct the first time and it won't take as long. At one stage in the process, I had each boy check over each other's work. If it wasn't going to pass JennJenn's approval, they had to redo it. The main goal was to carry these drilled-in lessons on past mama's nagging house—fingers crossed!

Now brace yourselves for this one. As many of the boys' friends may remember, or should I say, mostly Ethan's friends would remember, the JB was created during the early teen years. A JB is a "Jenn's Bitch" for the day. Yes, folks, you read that right. My boys would earn the title of JB, a.k.a. Jenn's Bitch, when they got into trouble. There was, on occasion, and trust me, it didn't happen often after the boys earned and suffered through the title of JB. Remember, we tried to find humor in every situation, and a JB gave us a good chuckle in what could have been a tense situation. An earned JB for the day was at my beck and call *all...day...long*. "Fold the laundry and put it all away." It was one chore after another. "Scrub all toilets in the house." No rest. Anything and everything that needed to be done around the house was added to the list. "Take out the trash." It was awful, but trust me, they got the message and were hardly ever in trouble, trouble. "Empty the dishwasher." But I do have to say, some weeks, it was simply put, awesome to have a JB to help get all the tasks around the house completed, when the work week just did me in. Really, did it hurt them? It was more likely their pee on the toilets, their constant food dishes in the dishwasher, and their endless piles of laundry. So if anything, it taught them to aim, reduce, and reuse!

It's amazing how years into the motherhood club tame you. What once would have been a complete humiliation or instant flip of a switch to a full-blown freak out will simply become a shrug or a sigh. One day, while at work, I got a text from our contractor when having some updates done in our house. Or should I say fixing around the house from the Timm boy abuse. "BTW [texting for dummies: by the way] there's a big sticky substance under your couch." I text back, "Of course there is. I'll deal with it when I get home. Thank you for letting me know." Later in the day, I pondered this earlier text:

1) Why wouldn't he just clean it up? He found it. *Men*!
2) Damn #$*&@#! kids. Which one did it?
3) How long could it have been there and no ants?
4) I bet I forget all about this mysterious stickiness when I get home and it's there for further months.

Because really, like I'm moving the couch anytime soon.

By the way (BTW), I did forget about that mysterious sticky substance by the time I got home from work and running a kid to a lesson or practice. A month or two later, when my men moved all the furniture out to play some great room basketball, I got the reminder. No ants, even they didn't want part of this pool of mystery. Winning. By then it was so unidentifiable we'll never know what it was. Of course, my man cleaned it up. Love him! No big deal, moving on to the next "shake my head" moment on this Timm ride.

Dropping your kiddos off to their friends' home always had me reminding them to say their pleases and thank yous. To be on their best behavior. Boys will be boys, but at least try. Please, for your JennJenn! But there was always something they would forget. My favorite one was a time I went to pick Evan, a preteen, up from a friend's house. He jumped into the truck:

Me: Hey, Evan (pause, scrunched-up, disgusted look). What's that smell?
Evan: Pee (very serious, looking out the window).
Me: What?
Evan: (Louder, clearer, and annoyed) *Pee*!
Me: Why do you smell like pee?
Evan: Because their dogs peed on my coat (again, serious, and like, duh).

Big Happy Chef smile. There you go. When I'm not around to remind him to hang up his coat for the hundredth time, a dog will do the reminder for me! Awe, payback is great. Yes, I have learned being a mama and laughing at such situations is a bit evil funny. Just pick up your damn coat like I taught you, told you, and begged you over and over! Lesson learned the hard way seems to always stick with them for the long haul more than Mama's constant nagging.

All through this ride, we and many others said the Timm reality show would have been a hit! We still kick ourselves that we didn't find a producer in the earlier years. No one would have believed the stuff that was said or went down. We couldn't make it up. I feel many mothers of boys could relate, or maybe many would sit stunned. Does this stuff really happen? Yep, this is life here. I tried to keep a tidy house, I tried to multitask, I tried to decorate for all the seasons, but I needed help. We had places to be, schedules were full, Mama was easily distracted, so all hands were on deck to help out and often ended up me barking orders to my Timm boys, bless their hearts.

Me: Hey, Ethan, could you please put this scarecrow out by the pumpkin on the front porch?

Ethan (in full 100 percent enthusiastic mode): Sure, I'll make it look awesome!

(Five minutes later, in passing) Me: So how does it look?

Ethan (giggling with excitement): He looks like he's tea bagging the pumpkin!

If you don't know what tea bagging is, I strongly advise you not to ask this question out loud or google this in a public place. Okay, I just googled in the privacy of my home while all the boys were sleeping so not too terribly bad, but still not advised in public. You have been warned! Oh, joys of raising boys…and yep, that scarecrow stayed that way all season. Again, find humor in all situations, or do as I did and just go numb a bit. I mean really, I wasn't specific enough. "Please put the scarecrow next to the pumpkin, on the front porch with his one arm around the pumpkin and the other arm nicely in his lap." Lesson learned, another rookie mom mistake. My bad!

Ethan gathered up some pussy willows from our backyard bush and put them in a vase for me. Then he renamed them Ryan willows…it just never stops!

Among our management schedules and the colorful coded calendar of activities, I was always doing home projects. I got this from my parents who remodeled or built a house every four years while I was growing up. It was part of my dad's construction business, so I was always around home improvements. Plus, my mom was into doing crafts and included us three kids from time to time. So we all carried this into our adult years. We were in full speed for our current project of updating all carpet to the matching laminate floor in our great room…or umm, mini basketball court room. Our plan was to do the flooring in stages over a couple of weeks, so it wasn't such an overwhelming maze of furniture in our one and a half story home. The goal was to do Evan's room and the loft first. Our pug, OLIVER! a.k.a Sir Shits-A-Lot, must have known this and left an abundant goodbye gift in the center of Evan's room. Exhausted, busy handling something else, and with no time to clean up thoroughly, I sent the Timm boys upstairs with a utility knife to cut out the gifted area and toss in the outside trash. Why not? We were going to rip it all up in a day or two later. What could go wrong? Yeah, I realize typing this now, why on earth would I give them a sharp utility knife and send them on their way! Once again, rookie mistake because the room was left with a big penis shape (testicles and all) cutout, front and center in the room!

The summer and holiday breaks for my boys were always such enjoyment—exhausted working mama sarcasm. They were too old for a sitter and too young for jobs, so home together it was, with always a nice chore list to keep them somewhat busy. I usually found myself dreading each last day of school before any summer or holiday break because it meant many things: may the house become a disaster, pantry and refrigerator be licked clean, invasion of numerous kiddos in the home, our wallets emptied, and tattling phone calls to work shall begin. Here we go again!

The day following an eventful lunch hour consisting of sarcastic, verbal, accusing, screaming fits between the boys, I make the decision to attempt another lunch at home to get a break from the office. I pulled into the driveway to see quite the array of overpriced and colorful bikes tossed in every direction. Because why would you use the bike stand attached to the bike? Obviously, a scratched-up bike would be way cooler. Anyway, this is a sure sign my house has been taken over by hormonal teenage boys. Sigh. Another fabulously, exhausting, stressful lunch at home is to be had. I take a deep breath and walk fast to the door to see if I would catch them in the act of doing anything of which I would disapprove because, as experienced, I'm sure it will be something. After slamming my face into the door, I realize this entry door that's always unlocked is *locked*. It's a sure sign that something is up and it's *not* good. Another sigh and debate. Do I just get back in my car and drive back to work or on to the next state? I knock, then pound, then frantically kick. All while I'm sure the neighbors are watching from their windows, enjoying their peaceful lunch and giggling as they watch this Timm Show in action. Finally, the little one, the twelve-year-old, answers the door. I push in hurriedly to catch something, anything in the act worthy enough to lock the door. I demand, screech, and scan the open floor plan. "Why is the door locked?" I asked to get the reply in an equally sounding response. "Because I just cleaned the whole house, and I didn't want Ethan's friends to come in and mess it up!" Stunned, shocked, this doesn't make sense. "What?" I spot Ethan and his friends camped out in the backyard, in the baking sun, all laying on the trampoline because the little one locked them out from demolishing the house and eating the pantry dry. Yep, we have learned a valuable lesson here, folks. Having the boys do all the chores during summer break has given them a whole new perspective on house respect after a good cleaning! Yes, I have patted myself on my back a lot in those days. Good job, JennJenn. It was another great reminder to not assume the worse. There are at times good intentions to what may be perceived as a devious situation.

One particular lovely Friday while Ethan and my Ryan were in Kansas City for a baseball tournament, the younger one, Evan, and I were planning to have a bonding weekend. I picked him up from school. He hops in the truck with a huge Happy Chef smile. Of course, as a good mama, I ask, "How was your day?" He responds, wait for it, "I saw a vagina today." Pause, shock. My eyes were large and bulging. Maybe I didn't hear him right. Remember, I don't always hear correctly. Surely I missed something.

Me: What?
Evan: A Va-J J or a kitty cat, whatever.

Uh, hello, teachers! Hello, school! I could have used a warning letter on that one to be prepared with a proper greeting on such subjects in school, or better yet, have traded spots with my Ryan for the pickup and handle! Instead, I was left shocked, uncomfortable, and handled it terribly all wrong. Imagine that. This was in junior high health class. They didn't do warning notes home first since it was part of the curriculum. They learned about tampons that day too. Lucky me. Hand to my face, with a deep sigh. I can't even put that conversation into reading words for such an audience. He is so like his father. We'll just tuck that conversation away as I think, *Holy balls, someone else can deal with that at a much later date!* We made it through the evening smoothly with no further awkward conversations. The following day, I left him alone for two minutes to check on my garden. Two minutes! When I came back in, he had drawn hair in his armpits with *permanent marker*! Yes, he was a normal sixth-grade boy, I kept reminding myself. Simply put, I drank a lot of wine in those days and repeated it out loud a lot. Just pick your battles.

One Saturday afternoon, we finally had a break in ball games, dance, family commitments, and plain old "we just want to be home" excuses. We thought this was the weekend to try out a new church. We checked a website for a new church in the area to attend their Sunday morning sermon. We set our alarms, woke up, showered, and dressed in our Sunday best, all with great attitudes and smiles to match. We headed out in the appropriate time to learn, yep, we read the website times wrong and have missed church entirely. It was even earlier than what our alarms were set for. On our slow drive back to our home, we looked at one another, and I made the comment, "Well, we're up and looking good. What shall we do?" My Ethan comments, seriously, "Darn, I was really looking forward to church." And the little one, Evan, comments in full character, "We tried. Let's head to the bar!" Sigh, inside laugh, roll my eyes at Ryan, who is chuckling and I'm sure contemplating some barbecue wings, a tall captain, and a little football as part of Evan's vision. I once again found myself questioning, "How on earth did I get myself such polar opposite children?"

At a bright 6:15 a.m. one school morning, as I was running around the house gathering all needed for the busy work day, dogs had water, breakfast dishes picked up, laundry switched and tumbling, I asked Ethan why he was all dressed up with a collared shirt and vest. He announced he had an art presentation but needed a tie. Again, 6:15 a.m., we have no ties nor time to recruit one. Here comes another sigh. Why on earth didn't he mention this last night during his thousand-word ramble? Too late. We got to go! At dinner that night, he announced he got two extra credit points on his presentation because he made himself a paper tie! Ha, that kid Jake no more. He's a genius! That boy will do just fine in life and can adapt to about any situation with that strong confidence, deep dimple smile, and contagious laugh. He even self-confirmed many years later on a weekend home visit from college, when he announced, "I'm a Joey Tribbiani and Ashton Kutcher combined!" Yes, my son, you truly are! You see, just try, give it your all, smile big, flash a little dimples, and laugh through any situation.

As a seasoned working mama, I learned very quickly in my boys' teen years that social media is my parenting friend. All I needed to do was one post from the office instead of dozen of phone calls: "Rumor has it there's a freshman party at our house this coming Saturday night. Let's get this clear: *there is no party at the Timm's!* We, and now Ethan included, won't even be home. So if your child says he's heading to the Timm's, ask twenty questions and put a stop to it! I'm debating on a police car being parked in the driveway, stadium lighting installed, and a security camera! Because we all know the dogs will welcome in anyone with chips!"

Call it lazy parenting, genius, or oh my word, what is going on over at the Timm's? I don't care. It got the job done. Word traveled fast; therefore, our house was just beautifully teepeed. They are so thoughtful. I was running low on our supply anyway. I was always grateful for the saved trips to the store from those accommodating teens! They did save us money in that area.

We tried. We honestly tried to do it all, balance it all, be on top of everything, but guess what! We got it wrong at times, we stumbled through at times, we offended and pissed others off at times. But we made it, everyone's alive, permanent marker does eventually fade away, and everyone's happy with many lessons learned. You see, just try, give it your all, don't care about the naysayers, smile big, flash a little dimples, and belly laugh through it. It truly is a chaotic but fun ride!

Just Say No

If you chase two rabbits, both will escape.
—Russian Proverb

There was a time we found ourselves caught up in life, signing up to be a part of everything. Both of us managers in our careers, attending meetings and group luncheons, running from work to attend local event meetings, running from meetings to attend school activities, running from activities to kids' lessons or to coach a sport. We were running, running, running. The house became a dumping ground. We relied on Post-it notes to keep it straight where everyone was. We were high fiving and texting each other in passing. The house was in disarray. We found ourselves eating later and later every night, only to start over doing the exact same joyride the next day. We lived out in the public and wanted to be a part of everything. And it seemed everywhere we were, more help was needed and being requested. It was all new and exciting, and the folks we were meeting made it all worth it. But then we just decided, enough is enough. We can't keep this up!

We got to the point that we just didn't make eye contact with anyone and changed our phone numbers. Kidding. But we did find our *no*. We said *no*! We learned to say *no*. In time we liked saying *no*. But within reason. A yes can be desired from time to time. A yes is nice when your talents are truly put to work. You don't need to run around saying yes to everything in sight until you have no time for yourself, are stressed out, overworked, leaving your family missing you and the house in complete dishevelment. Many groups and organizations could use your talents, and it takes volunteers to jump in for a successful outcome. Just learn to align yourself with your passions. It took us awhile to find our balance. But we did in time and hope younger families find it sooner than we did.

What is your talent or passion to share with others? That is the big question in life that we are all running around, trying to find the answer to at every age. Once you feel you have it figured out, *pow*, you're on a different path. Many voices may give you hints throughout the years, so pay attention. Once, my boys' wonderful day care providers' husband said to me, "You have more creativity in your little pinky than I have in my whole body." Hmm, the pressure is on. How can I use that to help others? What was meant as a compliment left me wondering and frantically searching. Now what do I do with this new information?

Around the boys' early teen years, I found myself in a sudden urge to purge our home of these silly things collecting dust. These money-wasting things. Why on earth would I have a basket of pine cones in front of my fireplace just sitting there doing nothing? To be dragged out by the furbabies on a constant routine. Do they bring me joy? No. Are they a treasured gift? No. Nor were they useful. They were just sitting there, calling for my time to be dusted on a weekly basis. Guess what, I learned to say *no*! No more unnecessary stuff. Surround yourself and spend your time on things that bring you joy, that use your talents, that ignite your passion, that tell your story. It took a few tragic news events and family hiccups through the years for my eyes to open to the larger picture on this journey. All the extras seemed nothing more than just silliness. Silly, silly, wasted money, stuff, and time.

We got to the point one year after a horrible loss of our furbaby, Ed, that we woke up and said enough was enough. No more excuses. We went out and bought ourselves an acreage with a much-desired downsized home; a fixer-upper. We had dreamed and talked about it for years. It was the fresh start we all needed, as our schedules calmed down. The projects and plans on which to refocus our attention as a family. Therefore, The Zen Ranch was established in August 2014. Three acres with an outdated fifties-style ranch home that needed a good overhaul. We fell in love with it instantly and could see the potential for our family. There never seemed a good time to do it before since we were caught up in our busy lifestyle. It was to the point if we didn't do it now, we may never do it. We did it on Evan's freshman and Ethan's junior year of high school! We said *no* to our keeping up with the Joneses' neighborhood lifestyle and *yes* to our dream, to family time of creating a home, and to a life we didn't need a vacation from.

I'm sure we got the whole town talking, leaving a huge, newer home for a little fifties faded mint green ranch home complete with shag carpet, pink stoned fireplace, orange kitchen cabinets, rotting windows, and rooster-covered wallpaper. This new place to be called home was embarrassingly named the Crack House by the Timm boys. We sold, donated, or left much of our furniture and things—our stuff. It was the ultimate awesomeness to complete our boys' last years' home with us as a family. We got their imagination involved in the remodeling process which created an appreciation and togetherness among our entire family. Yes, we planted a few Ryan willows around the property too! (The Zen Ranch, a whole other book brewing.) We learned to say *no* to the things we didn't enjoy or desire and *yes* to a life that felt like we were on vacation from the time we pulled in the driveway. The goal was to create a life we didn't need a vacation from, and that we accomplished.

Come together as a family. Claim your goals and work hard to achieve them with full force. Ignore what others think of your chaos. This is your ride. Tackle your bucket list with determination. Make all your dreams come true because you get one chance at this ride. Make it an amazing one no matter which direction it takes you!

Suburban Mama What the Hell

A Journey to Find You

Ride 1.5

Ride 1.5

I'm hard of hearing and socially awkward with a handful of bitchiness. What's not to love? I stand together with Carrie Bradshaw, "I'd rather be someone's shot of whiskey than everyone's cup of tea"!

Life is bumpy, sticky, and messy. Learn to jump in, grip tight, and enjoy your ride, yelling yeehaw the whole time!

She's All Over the Map

Just remember, not all who wander are lost.
—J.R.R. Tolkien

*M*e described in words by my sister, many, many years ago, was unique. Quite possibly viewed by others as weird, different, and strange. My words for myself, as put in a book assignment in college, were *sassy, dreamer, spirited, mysterious,* and *creative.* Later in my working adult life suspected as *opinionated, confusing, impatient, moody, driven* (to do my own thing). It's funny. As I look at each of these words by my sister, others, and by myself, they describe my younger son, Evan, exactly. He is my own duplicate, so I can see me in a new light. It's an awesome view at times, and other times I feel for him. I've struggled with the list of words from time to time. I think it's good to make these lists through the years on how you view yourself. Maybe even paying close attention to how others describe you. These words are not always meant in a bad way. My sister made it very clear that her description of *unique* was viewed as creative, standing out in the crowd, and drumming to my own beat. And she assured me it was inspiring to her and others. I think everyone should get busy making your list of words to describe you. Tuck that list away, bring it out from time to time, and add to it. Find *you* in those words.

My Evan and I were born in the year of the dragon. According to the Chinese calendar, the dragon will launch straight into projects or conversations with a pioneering spirit. Dragons often fail to notice others trying to keep up or indeed those plotting behind their backs (maybe because we could give a rat's ass). As authority figures, they make their own laws and cannot bear restrictions. They prefer to get on with a job themselves and are good at motivating others into action—sometimes, with snide/sarcastic comments. Yes, us dragons!

Dragons are always available to help others, but their pride makes it difficult for them to accept help in return. Although they are always at the center of things, they tend to be loners (gasp, there's that ugly word again!) and are prone to stress when life becomes difficult. Hardworking and generous, they enjoy excitement and new situations. When upset, they can be explosive, but all soon forgotten.

Well, folks, this description or warning label of me would have been very useful years ago. Maybe this description should have been attached to me when I arrived on this great ride. My coworkers, through the years, could have used this as a bio when working with me to understand. "Oh, she was born the year of the dragon. We understand now."

The year of the dragon is fitting given the first tattoo I got randomly at eighteen years of age was a dragon. Coincidence? I think not! See, Mama, it was not worth freaking out about. It was meant for me! When I look back at that scene of the new tattoo reveal to my mother, it was a bit of a hilarious episode. Apparently, she misunderstood me thinking it was a delicate one-inch flower under the bandage. Obviously, she was quite surprised when the bandage was removed several days later to reveal a black, tribal, and a bit larger than thought dragon tattoo.

I encourage all who are struggling to understand your own behaviors, attitudes, and feelings to go eat at a Chinese restaurant today and read the paper place mat to find your warning label.

When dabbling *me* a bit further in a feng shui book years ago, I learned in the Five Elements Chart that I was fire. Fire people are leaders (check) and crave action (I do like an adventure). They inspire others to follow (because really, are you going to say no to a dragon?), often in trouble (moi?) as they dislike rules (or being bossed/mothered), and fail to see consequences (no major trouble—yet!). Positively they are innovative (creatively hardworking folk), humorous (it's a gift from the big guy above), and passionate people (awe, shucks). Negatively they are impatient (a gene from my father, but then there's Mother—double whammy), exploit others, and have little thought for their feelings (oops, yes, been there, done that! A sincere apology to you and you and you over there!)

I once had a personalized color analysis done. This was a pretty neat experience. The goal is to discover the rainbow connection between color and your character. The color computer tells you about your personality, moods, and feelings. By putting select colors in order, it will determine you. My sequence suggested I was desirous of a life free from conflict and stress (I'm working hard on this). I'm a strong person with determination to win, even against heavy odds (yeah, I'll show you. Sit back and watch. I got this!). I see myself as a unique person (umm, wasn't that my sister who said that, not me?) and enjoy being recognized (uh yeah, I've done the work; give me credit). I feel I have been prevented from achieving the success I desire and in no way will accept this as a final outcome for my personal accomplishments (yep, I've got even more planned for this trip. I feel it!). I am optimistic. I will prevail. I am determined to succeed at all costs. Through self-belief and action, everyone succeeds.

Feeling curious of you, your feelings, and personality? Study, dabble, search, and ask away. There's much information out there. Just get creative in your search. It's fun and will help you determine the *you* you were meant to be!

I felt for a long time I have had to explain myself, to transform, to fit in. To disguise myself to be the norm and to hide. To not be pointed out or found out. To try to fit their mold. What have I discovered along the way? Who gives a shit! Be you—the person that you are designed to be. Let it shine through; don't fight it. You get one chance at this ride. Enjoy it and do what makes you happy. I'll say it proud now: "I'm a unique loner and perfectly content to be one!"

My man, Ryan, gave me a Dr. Seuss saying (gosh, he is wonderful) several years back. I had it posted in my bathroom for years, to stare at every morning before I step out into this crazy world: "Be who you are and say what you feel, because those who mind *don't* matter and those who *matter* don't mind." Ha, in your face! What a great motto to live by. Even after a bottle of wine, really, they don't mind what just spewed out of your mouth. Your tribe gets you or shakes their heads at you or calls you out on your crap. I love each one of you who *matter* to me! Find those that matter in your life. Surround yourself with them—those who encourage you, lift you, and inspire you. Embrace them and cherish them, because they are very hard to come by. Although you must remember not to "put foot in mouth" when saying what you feel too much, which I am certainly guilty of a time or ten. Make the words count. Be *T*rue, *H*elpful, *I*nspiring, *N*ecessary, and *K*ind: THINK before you open that big mouth. I had it tattooed on my wrist to remind myself of this daily and often struggle to comply with it.

Stay positive. It's hard to do sometimes. Well, a lot of times. Especially when saying what you feel may come out judgmental, opinionated, or downright bitchy! But if you surround yourself with those that matter, who get you, they really won't mind and always understand in time what you meant. Negativity spreads negativity, and it's a nasty state to live in. I know, I was there for a number of years. Looking back, how foolish it was. It sucked. What a waste of time, energy, and relationships. Obviously, more naps were needed in those days. A little sleep always recharges the mind and soul! Well, that, and quite possibly less wine.

I've Got Plans for Myself So Get Out of My Damn Way

Ten years from now, make sure you can say
you chose your life; you didn't settle for it.
—Mandy Hale

There was a time around my late twenties when I felt I was leading a selfish, negative life. I had lost myself on this journey. Ryan and I weren't in a good place. I was tired and annoyed with my young family, my work, and my life in general. I was not a good friend, mother, or wife. I was angry, restless, and depressed. I had never come from a church family. God was not mentioned on a regular basis in my home, nor did I really believe there was one. One day, I was in one of my usual mopey moods, sitting at the kitchen table with no husband or boys around. I'm sure they were hiding from my ugliness. I was mindlessly flipping through the local newspaper when a church flier fell into my lap. It changed everything. I felt this sudden urge to check it out and learn more. It was a wake-up call or slap across the face: Hello, come on in and check us out! So I did. I, of course, was greeted with open arms.

I attended those first several months with just our young boys. I was learning as much as I could. I was reading as much as I could. I invited the pastor's wife over to explain what I was reading and attended weekly Bible studies. I just couldn't get enough; it was so new to me and exciting. In time, Ryan started joining us, as he saw quite the renewed spirit in me. I started reading the Bible. It took me three years to read, but I did read it cover to cover. I reread portions and charted out families, and I completed this goal I placed for myself. We became members of the church. I got baptized, relearned to laugh at the humor of life, and realized when the big guy upstairs had taught me a lesson. I slowed down and learned to listen, accept, appreciate, and love.

The church dissolved over the years, and from time to time I do think of that small church that I felt was created to pull me back where I was meant to be. For that I will be forever thankful to that little marketing flier that fell into my lap that sad, sorry day, and to the church family who so kindly took us in to help guide us back. Now here's hoping a similar flier will fall into your lap when needed most.

Later, in my early thirties, I remembered thinking I had been a wife coming up on eleven years, a mother to a seven- and nine-year-old, and yet hadn't I taken the time to stop, breathe, and connect. Why haven't I slowed down and pondered my journey? Where has the time gone? Have I lost sight of me again? I encourage you all as you read this to do just that: slow down and enjoy. Don't be so serious. Stop to give high fives, hugs, kisses, and pats on the backs to your children, your husband, your friends, and your coworkers. Okay, maybe not kisses to your coworkers, because that is just weird (not the good, encouraged creative weird), and you could end up with a sexual harassment lawsuit on your hands. Unless you marry your coworker like I did twenty-plus years ago! Good luck with that. This life is too short. The years your children are in your home will fly by, and your spouse should feel needed, appreciated, and valued.

In my late thirties, I watched a young gal's life unfold on social media. She was a college student of a baseball family we had grown to know very well through the years. I felt drawn to her, to reach out as I knew and felt at one time, exactly what she was going through. I gave her a tip that worked for me. "When I was your age, I made a dream/goal board, and it was the best thing I did. I still have one and add to it through the years. Basically, it's a foam core board with photos and sayings to inspire *me*, what I want to be, what I would like out of this life, for my family, for my relationships, for my sanity. I have it in an area where I can view it, ponder it—to keep me on track. I also put inspiring messages all around me to keep me happy, healthy, and trucking forward. Give it a try and see what it brings you! This is your life. Live it like you want it to be, and don't let anyone get in your way! In time you just won't care what people think of you. I remember the feelings you are going through until a wise, experienced lady and a professional in our community told me in a firm voice, *'Fuck them!'* Life will throw you many bad things constantly. It sucks at the time, and times you'll want to throw in the towel and run away. But it is what it is, and how we react to it sets the tone. I say laugh it off, buck up, and tackle it, yelling 'Yeehaw' the whole ride! I'm here for you, gal, and so is your family. Don't be around people who bring negative feelings your way. Take control and surround yourself with positive, good people for you. It's your life. Make a list of what you want out of it. Those people don't belong on it. Ignore them, get away from them. They aren't there nor exist in your life anymore. Put your foot down and say '*No, you can't treat me that way. I won't accept it!*' You are a beautiful person, and in time you will find that boy who will see it. Be patient and don't rush it! I'm telling you, it's worth the wait."

I saw many "make me smile" posts from this gal after that day. She was on her way, and she soon found her "Sackin' Fish" and, not long after, celebrated their growing family. What a blessing of a ride!

> *Don't let your* dreams *be dreams.*
> —Jack Johnson

In my thirties, I was creating and selling playtime creations, so I decided to create a social media page and logo with my dad's nickname for me: Furbag. I have to tell you, because it makes me giggle coming from the source. Soon after I posted this page and logo for all to see, my mom quickly emailed me, saying she didn't think my creation's name Furbag sounded bohemian or whimsical for my items (she proceeded to make suggestions of new names). I said no firmly to any thought of changing the name because I always wanted to use this nickname for my creations. She pointed out the name reminded her of an old lady's crotch hairs! What! Why on earth would she allow my father to call me that name for years and years (and still does) if that is what it reminded her of? I'm dying, laughing, my hand to my forehead, shaking my head, and I'm sure you all are too! What the hell is wrong with my mother?

What's a Furbag, you ask. Well, it's *me*, JennJenn! My father has always called me Furbag. It was his way of showing attention in his manly way. It wasn't until my mid-thirties did I know why he called me this. I had always thought it was Furbag with a *U*. I assumed because he also called us three kids varmints. While on a trip through Europe as an adult with my parents, I learned that it was meant as Ferbag, as in JenniFER. And in his eyes, I dressed like a bag lady through my teen years. After this laugh, we shared, I had *Furbag* tattooed on the top of my foot, facing me so I can see it all the time. To this day, I still giggle and tear up every time I see it. When my father first saw this tattoo, he did as well. I *love* this name! It means something very special to me. It is sassy, mysterious, quirky, spirited, unique, and fun, like my creations at the time! I am and will always be his Furbag!

During this time of Furbag's creative playtime, I had to remind myself and many others that yes, of course I still have my full-time day career. But we all have our own passions and hobbies outside of our day job and must explore our passions to grow, relieve stress, and escape too! My passion has always been recycling, drinking wine, and designing. Therefore, Furbag began its journey. I sold many, but it's not like I made any money on it. I recycled it all back in on the fun. It was Zen Jenn's fun time! This gal can chaotically multitask, loves projects, always up to the challenge to try new things, and is notorious for taking on way too much. With my Timm men behind me, I skipped and giggled my way through that adventure as well. It lasted a good year or so of dabbling in craft shows, selling in local shops, and had my own rented booth in a rather large vendor rental store, but then it became more than I wanted to put into it at the time and soon became interested in another focus (squirrel!).

Continue to feed your soul! Go ahead and let others shake their heads. It's their loss if they don't take that leap of their own passions and wander. It's perfectly okay to jump from interest to interest. It helps define what is really important to you and what is not.

My Days Are Spent at the Circus

The difference between who you are and
who you want to be is what you do!
—Bill Phillips

In this journey, we start getting titled, grouped, or defined as to what we will be or do. We may even be told regularly as what to become professionally. Or we were directed toward the correct career path to wander down. For me, I always knew it would be something associated with art or design. I remember rearranging my room on a regular basis at a young age. I remember decorating or staging classrooms in my head while sitting in class in grade school. I was awarded several titles, certificates, ribbons, and achievements for poster design contests from grade school through college. I had felt at times like I gave up on me by diving into marriage and family so early in the journey. I go full force before I burn myself out and rethink a situation. I feel many of us mothers at times question this—the what ifs. Do we just cast aside our passions? Do we need a paper certificate, commission check, or a plaque to define who we are? Hell no.

My interests have jumped through the years. I find excuses to change. Maybe I get that "been there, done that" feeling too quickly. What it boils down to be is that life is short; let's try something else now. I find myself easily bored yet easily entertained and intrigued by a new adventure. I am a diligent worker and creative, so I jump in pretty hard with such enthusiasm that when others don't join in with me on the journey, I quickly burn out and usually run from the situation…maybe even be a bit more dramatic and burn that darn bridge for a grand finale.

It would occur to me that I had this ideal me, the person I wanted to be, and yet I would do the complete opposite. As read in the book of Proverbs and book of James— what a fool we are! At times I would feel that I was on this crazy carnival swing, going in all directions, not able to steady myself and stay in one direction. Sometimes I would hear Ryan's voice: "Is this it? Is this what you want to do? Are you going to stick with it?" Silly man. Has he learned nothing through the years? Possibly not! Just do it, dive in, and try something new and exciting. This is your chance. Find what you love to do and do it! So what would that be? I assure you, you will figure it out. Be patient; it takes time, and there's a process to this journey.

After college, I worked a few years as a desktop publisher in a nine-to-five cubicle being told what to do all day, every day. I quickly realized this was not what I wanted to do. Remember, I'm a dragon. We don't like being told what to do. After a year's stint at a day care center with my Ethan, then a few years home with my young boys, I went back to the workforce. We realized I was a better away from the home as a working mom than an at-home-mom. I didn't make much money after paying off day care at the end of the week, but I thoroughly enjoyed the time I was an in-home custom decorating consultant for a nationwide home décor store. It gave me the opportunity to explore my creative side. It got me showered, dressed up, and out of the house. A little bling and some heels does wonders for a gal (by now surrounded by boys, boys, and boys, I found a touch of my girly side). Although I felt at the time restricted to just selling custom window treatments and pillows. So I stepped it up and had great success as one of the top territory sellers since I gave these scheduled clients the added touch of additional suggestions to pull their room together, which normally led to more rooms in their homes. Come on, really, you question I was going to hold back from telling my clients what I really thought? This honest opinion landed me many side gigs by such clients to take their space to the next level as well. The career was fun, rewarding, and truly a thrill with my sales always on the high end. Therefore, my commission checks reflected my hard work. In due time, the lagging economy started affecting the whole trip, and carrying numerous sample books in and out of appointments in all-weather elements took a toll on my body. Damn it!

I eventually found a long-term position through some neighbors at their custom vinyl graphic company. This new position combined my sales and design skills in an equally rewarding adventure. There was something new and exciting every single day. The days consisted of deadline rushes, balancing department schedules to client schedules, and a nice mix of sitting down in an office setting plus being out and about and meeting clients whenever I wanted to. Before I knew it, I found myself there for ten-plus years, earning myself my own office, a company vehicle, a fancy title, and maybe a few more wrinkles, gray hairs, and sleepless nights. But what a thrill it was!

Life in the world of sales:
It all works out—after we can't sleep or breathe, have
a constant vomiting feel and an ulcer brewing—when
our incentive checks, a new client referral or a proud
testimonial email from our clients erases any ill feelings.

During those high rush days, I found I was treating myself at the local nail salon on a regular basis. Nothing like ending a completely long, stressful office day in the life of sales with a manicure and a spa pedicure, only to have the size zero gal eagerly say, "I wax your lip?" (#throwinginthe-towel). Have you ever envisioned kicking these gals while they have your foot in their delicate little hands? All while the ladies sitting next to you giggle a bit because yeah, they weren't the only ones who got the suggestion. This is one of those "breathe, just breathe, and let it go" moments. Yes, ma'am, I'll take that glass of wine now!

I went through a few turbulent times at this position. I loved the job, the clients, and the thrill of deadlines, but sometimes working with others who seemed to get off by creating chaos for others had me in complete dragon mode.

And honestly, at times, we all just get tired of some folks' shit. As a grown woman and mother of teenagers with a professional title, I once sent a random email to my parents after a much heated day in the office. Still to this day, I giggle over it. Yes, I said *giggle* because I can't remember why I was so upset. What could have been so horrible to send such an email as an adult to my parents? "I say you just give me my inheritance now so I can stay home before I murder someone and you have to use all of our inheritance to help Ryan with lawyer fees to keep me out of prison! It's just a thought for a more peaceful, zen, harmonious life for us all!" I may have been a bit dramatic. Oh well, those times have passed. All is golden, and my inheritance is saved. (Right, still there?)

Laugh and shake your heads at such silly road blocks in your ride. We all have them. We're all struggling a bit and are trying to get it all right. Many lessons are learned, maybe a few moments you wish you could redo or explain yourself better, but honestly just chuck it in the F-it bucket, move on, and do better on the next round.

The Freak Show

The problem is not the problem. The problem
is your attitude about the problem.
—Captain Jack Sparrow

Okay, folks, this chapter may be a bit much for some and a bit too much information for others. If you are shocked or blush easily, proceed at your own risk. If you are a male reading this book, you may want to skip over this chapter. Or if you want to be in tune with your lady partner and understand what she is going through, by all means read on. I did warn you! Brace yourself because yes, I am actually sharing this! No one, but no one, prepared me for this. Someone may thank me one day for sharing such personal details as they, too, once felt like a freak of nature during and several years after the kiddos had arrived. To my boys, you did this. Read it so you understand why I freaked out at times and can help your woman friends through this someday.

Being pregnant is the most beautiful, lovely, and glowing experience a woman could go through. *Bull crap*! Pregnancy was the most disgusting, smelly, tiring, sweaty experience I have gone through. Twice! If I wasn't feeling as if I was going to lose my breakfast, snack, lunch, or last year's holiday meal on someone at any moment, I was leaking fluids from every crevice of my body. You name it, it leaked. It was a constant moist. I know we all just love that word, feeling everywhere for nine months and several months after. Yep, freaking gross, and no one shares this until years later after a few drinks and doing pregnancy comparisons. Sisterhood my ass! I remember even my mouth not working correctly, and most of my food ended up on my shirt or lap. Don't worry, I didn't let anything go to waste. I'm pretty sure I licked or sucked every last flavor out of my clothing.

You're this bloated creature, hobbling around or laying around like a beached whale, ready to explode from either end at any moment. Don't get me wrong, you're not going to explode with a much needed BM because, honey, that only happened on blessed occasions. But explode like your man's morning routine just rising from the bed. And don't even get me started on the cluster of bulging hemorrhoids you get. Get the picture? I just want to be honest about how it really is. When the time does finally arrive, you may be mistaken for the first several hours of having bad gas pains and hide in the theater restroom for fear of ripping one off in a quiet movie. Fine, that could have only happened to me. (*Water Boy* with Adam Sandler. I'm sure you were curious.) We laugh about it now, and now shall you. I'm here to share. You're welcome!

When you actually get admitted to the hospital, you get a revolving door of nurses and med students coming in to watch the freak show of this bloated, sweaty, food-stained, and now freaking out female. With my first son, I had the pure pleasure of hiding out in the tiny hospital shower to calm down so that I would dilate. Once the show was actually in progress in the wee hours of the morning, the nurse had the doctor paged. The doctor entered the room in a sleep-deprived slumber. He was stumbling around with his footsies and trying to read the stats. Ryan and I had never seen such a madhouse as the nurse ripped the paperwork out of the doc's hands and pushed him toward my open legs, screaming, "I will tell you what's in the chart. She's having a baby!" That's when you will know the nurses are running the show. She was in my face as a vicious, evil, screaming, spitting commander to push! I realize now I met my dragon match. Of course, I could only concentrate on this "OMG [texting for dummies: oh my god], I'm ripping apart" feeling down below. I had forgotten to breathe. Not having had an epidural, I went into complete shutdown mode. I was *done.* Twenty-two years old and didn't want to be in this environment or situation anymore. I took myself somewhere else and laid back, ignoring all around me. The doctor looked at me, the nurse, and poor Ryan. My Ryan had to reaffirm, "She's done." Yep, I'm that darn stubborn. Remember, I'm a dragon. We don't listen to anyone telling us what to do. My Ethan was delivered with the help of forceps and vacuum, sporting a nice cone head for the first hour or so. The evidence of me not using the recommended breathing skills showed up several hours later. I was styling with broken blood vessels all around my eyes. With the second child, we were fortunate enough to have a due date around Thanksgiving. Therefore, I was a bit persuaded to be induced to accommodate my doctor being home for the holidays with his family. We all know I hate surprises anyway, so let's just get the show on the road and skip all the previous hassles. Being induced is this lovely feeling of constantly peeing yourself while lying in a bed, leaving your husband to change the towels and bedding under you while the understaffed nurses are preoccupied with other divas in rooms down the hall. Thank goodness, after my first lovely experience, I just wanted to be left alone in a corner to curl up and ignore once again what was about to happen to my body. I had Ryan across the room taking in a game on the television, yelling out from time to time, "You doing okay?" I shouldn't complain at all about my deliveries. Both boys arrived in four hours of actual labor time— the big guy upstairs understands me. I have such respect to you twenty plus-hour labor gals. You women are *rock stars*!

After the lovely delivery, they send you home with this new, little, beautiful creature, a bag full of sexy mesh granny panties, and three-inch thick "belly button to butt crack" pads. They will remind you to ice the swollen and stitched-up, abused area down below and behind. Yes, sweetheart, you may rip and rip terribly. *No one tells you this!*

Nor did anyone ever mention to me to ice my swollen and hard bosoms if not breastfeeding. I proudly chose not to breastfeed. I told you, I was so done with the entire experience. I wanted my body back, and honestly, I deserved a tall glass of wine from the shock of the whole experience. The morning I woke up with hard, terribly sore bosoms, I called my mom right away. That women deserves a cape.

Mom to the rescue! She suggested bagged frozen peas on each breast. Of course, being young and freshly new parents, we had no such thing in our freezer, but we did have plenty of deer meat from my mighty hunter dad—that left my white bra stained with bright-red ink: *Property of Dennis Collins*! Remember, I hated to shop, so I wore that stained bra for a good few years. Giggle, giggle.

After the lovely shutdown experience during my first delivery and blowing all the blood vessels in my face, it became evident later that I also did damage to my hearing. We didn't notice this for some time later, as all we heard was crying the first couple of years. Remember, my first child, Ethan, was colicky. It was lovely; thumbs up. The loss of hearing wasn't in just one ear but both. And it seemed to get worse with each passing year. Even with my hearing aids, I struggled to hear. It was a blessing and a curse through the years. But let's just say Ryan got up most nights with the boys, not only because he is an amazing man but because he actually heard them!

Let's face it, we gals are blessed with the dreaded monthly Aunt Flo. By my late twenties, we started noticing a huge difference in my monthly event. Yeah, I said *we* (my house of males, friends, extended family, coworkers, quite possibly the mailman too). It was that big of a notice. An ob-gyn will tell you, "If you have a blood clot bigger than a quarter, you should call in." A quarter? Umm, mine were the size of a clementine. It was like an avalanche. I felt it drop, I felt my face go white, and I would feel weak. This went on for about a year. I couldn't leave the house one day out of a month in fear of erupting in public. I would put two pads on and sometimes a diaper just to hold it all in for half an hour at a time. It was awful. Yeah, I know, awful gross to read too. But I found out sharing my experience after enduring this for a year that other women have had similar experiences! Who knew? What the hell, gals, you are to share this bit of information so we don't feel like a freak show! Anyway, moving on. One night, after a quick trip to the store, even though I told my Ryan it wasn't good timing or a good idea given my situation that day, he realized from the "I told you so" evidence all over his truck seat that we needed to do something. An ablation (cauterizing of the uterus) was performed after much consultation. I already had my tubes cut/sealed/tied—a sealed deal. I had this procedure immediately after our second child, Evan, arrived. In fact, I think I screamed, "Tie me up, tie me up now!" I knew I was done but wanted my Ryan, in the event that something happened to me, to have the opportunity to give his second wife a child, if desired. (You are welcome. Hope your baby is colicky too!) Now, gals, an ablation is a true blessing. Some may spot a little during their monthly showdown. I was extremely thankful with absolutely nothing each month for five whole blessed years. Hallelujah! And yes, I bragged about this to *everyone*.

Okay, moving on to another thing no one talked about. But later, after hidden embarrassing moments, I learned many have struggled too. Once again, I'll man up to share so you know you are not alone in this mommy adventure. In my early thirties, I noticed leaking. I couldn't explain it, just leaking. I was also always running to the restroom, bathroom, sink, shower, pool, rock—whatever I could pee anywhere! In fact, for some odd reason, my sister has many of these pictures in her phone. If you give her enough drinks, she may even show them. Yep, it happened a few times. This led me once again back in to the woman doctor, then on to an urologist for medication, an ultrasound, then to be rewarded with a bladder test. Oh, sweet baby Jesus, no one and I mean no one even prepared me for this experience! Sure, why not, pull up a chair and watch. Oh, the humility! And that's exactly how the appointment went. A female was assigned to fill your bladder while you sat on a potty chair, legs spread, while she watched all coming out and chart it. I wanted a bag over my head. I wanted to run, but I couldn't out of fear of peeing myself. Obviously, this poor women did something terribly wrong in her career to be assigned to this awful duty. She was a lovely lady. I got to know her well during that appointment. She smelled good too. Anyway, a bladder mesh sling procedure was performed. Don't worry, folks, it was a better version than what was all over television with the lawsuits. So far so good (knock on wood).

Immediately after this procedure, and I mean immediately after, my normal bowel issues escalated out of control. When I went home from the hospital with my babies, I also went home with constant bowel issues and was on a prescription strength laxative. Anal fissures had happened from time to time too. Look it up and read others' descriptions. They are awful, like a nasty paper cut in the anus. Umm, yeah, a "bite down on a towel" ouchy experience. More likely the newest situation stirred from the recent bladder sling procedure and medications. But I got an anal fissure that just wouldn't heal and got bigger and bigger. Then the muscle (I'm not explaining anymore, you understand) was so inflamed that it wouldn't release. I would rather pass two babies at once out of my vagina with no pain medications before going through this experience ever again. It makes me tear up, and I have a vomiting feeling just thinking about it, so I'll breeze through this one as fast as I can. Anyway, I was on medications, in and out of the ass doctor's office (sorry, that's what is in my cell phone, just can't remember the correct type of doctor and too tired to look it up.) After a situation of me lying on the floor of my office; having to be picked up by a coworker and my Ryan to be helped to our truck, in pain for days at home; Ryan repeatedly calling the doctor's office, begging for help and a desperate make-it-stop ice cube shoved in my crack performance to attempt to numb the pain. I'm trying to just get through this section with Lamaze breathing as it's bringing back memories of the knife-from-a-fire, slicing-up-my-ass feeling all over again. The ass doctor quickly canceled her vacation and scheduled an emergency surgery the next morning. Thank God!

Now try to explain all that to your male-dominated workplace and why you are missing work. Even better, after home from that surgery, the day I was to return to work, I woke up with the whole left side of my body spasming and tight. I could hardly move and was once again in pain and tears. Guess the whole week of stress and trauma had my muscles in a lurch. Gratefully, I got to stall a few more days of explaining my absence at work with some much-needed muscle relaxers. *Amen.*

Friends, coworkers, and family were wonderful and humorous during this time. We learned our Evan would never cut it as a nurse, ever. And dear Ethan and his constant entourage of friends have absolutely no boundaries, as they would crawl in bed with me to watch television. Wine was the best cure/gift for these type of situations. We were impressed to learn that there are appropriate/worded greeting cards for truly anything. Of course, my Ryan was awesome. He's once again tea making, back rubbing, steam mopping, chick-flick getting kind of man. He's my Sackin' Fish!

Life continued, and I stayed out of the doctor's offices for about a year before the leaking returned and bloating, pain, and other lovelies appeared. Here I go again. I did my rounds of doctor visits. I was relieved to learn the bladder mesh sling was all good. It appears my uterus was full of a mystery fluid and a couple of polyps. A partial hysterectomy was needed. Because I'm me and this was another huge inconvenience in my life, I stalled this surgery until it fit my schedule and may have pushed it a month too long. This time around, I was at the point of not caring who knew my business. I just came out and said to my male boss the details, and off to the surgery and home for six weeks I went, with a male, awkward, uncomfortable "take all the time you need" code for don't talk private girl talk out loud to me again. No really, my work was wonderful and understanding.

On a plus side, after those scares, fiascos, and downtimes, equaled a twenty-pound weight gain, I was quickly back to our busy family schedule, day job, and down to a fabulous, rocking jean size. So *booyah*. All sunshine, zen time, and rainbow feelings here on out.

Deal with it and move on. We are women. Hear us roar. We can handle anything with a good support circle, stylish lounge wear from your mama, and a great attitude. Whew, we got through this. On to more of the ride.

Betty Crocker She Is Not

I think I'll just stay out of the kitchen.
—JennJenn

I honestly can say I have no idea what to do in this department. I never learned or desired the skill. Food never was that important to me to take the time to think about preparing it. I honestly could just make do with anything in front of me. My mom was even this way; therefore, popcorn and malts was not unusual for a dinner during my childhood. Thankfully, my man came from a household where the men cooked; another blessing in my life. I was told from the start of our living arrangement, "Let's just leave the meals to me." No argument from this gal. Just do your thing, honey.

I do contribute during birthdays, parties, or holidays. Desserts are ordered and picked up. They are all nicely decorated and packaged, and I continue to love my clean, "still looking brand-new" oven through the years. Not sure why everyone gets so stressed around such events. Just take the hassle out of it all and call in your order to your local bakeries. They are there to help!

My noncooking gene must have rubbed off on my oldest, Ethan. During his junior high years, he had to take a culinary class. He came home from school one day, all excited about a gluten-free recipe his teacher shared with him. He couldn't wait to cook it all by himself. I took him to the local grocery store to get all the ingredients because having a constant stocked house seemed to not be my thing either. He was so organized with his list of all the ingredients he needed. I sat away and worked on my laptop while he was in the kitchen, cooking away. Of course, he didn't want any assistance. He had it covered, like I would have been any help anyway. He finished and cleaned up after himself then sat down to devour five whole pancakes before saying, "JennJenn, does this taste funny to you?" He shoved a forkful toward me. Always happy to oblige, I immediately spit it out in disgust. I asked for the recipe then questioned what steps he did. I felt I could grasp what went terribly wrong. He used one-fourth *cups* of salt instead of the one-fourth *tsp*. He is such his mother's son! He tried, and that's all that counts. We laughed then he continued to eat the rest, but with added syrup to help the taste and gallons of water. We could always count on him to clean his plate entirely. Waste not, that child!

At one point in my late thirties, I had an epiphany that I was officially *awesome* and could do anything. Yes, I'm sure this occurred after a few glasses of wine and too much time on my hands. So I headed toward the room I'm rarely found in to accomplish a goal I had set for myself. With many raised eyebrows and concerned looks from my Timm men, I cooked about everything in my Pinterest

Gluten-Free album in one night. Yes, I said *I cooked.* It all looked amazing, with no fire alarms going off or cut fingers. The whole episode left one of my boys snapping pictures to show off on social media. One was shoveling in the food straight from the pans. No, not the boy who didn't mind the salted pancakes. Oh, the little things in life that brings smiles and warm fuzzy feelings. Well, that feeling left shortly after. Been there, done that. Cooking is handed back over to the man of the house. Now we all know I can do it without burning the house down. Well, at least that time.

Try stepping out of your norm from time to time. It could be a great thrill to try something new. If it doesn't work out, no harm done. Been there, done that, won't try again. Plus, sometimes you surprise the hell out of yourself!

Mama Likes a Party

Those were the days, my friend. Hydrate, Hydrate.
—Unknown

We all go through that phase and find ourselves letting loose, maybe a bit too much. I may have gotten this gene from my grandpa Dave. He was often quoted saying, "A good scotch cures anything—just have a scotch!" I also had no issue living up to this through my high school years and maybe a bit through my college years. Fine! Also several years into adulthood too! Nothing wrong with that; it's a time to sow your seeds and let your hair down a bit. You're just making some fun memories. Remember, I didn't find my *no* until much later in life. Giggle, giggle.

I set goals from time to time and strive to achieve or exceed these goals. One snowed-in winter morning with the worse hangover ever, I realized I needed a new goal to work toward, and the obvious presented itself: let's see how long I can go without an adult beverage. Let's not put a time limit on this. I'm really not that kind of gal.

I realized this new goal I set for myself was going to be a bit more of an obstacle when my own mother said,

"No, Jennifer, you like your drinks. Just limit yourself." An AA mentor she would not be, and the reactions from our friends at that time was a crowd silencing "Nooooooooo!" At one point, it became quite a debate among four couples on how I should rework this goal and just modify the number of drinks. One gal yelled out to my Ryan, "She's broken. You need to fix her!" But I had my mind set, and I was going to do this. I had said it out loud, so it was on! Guess what. I had remembered all conversations very clearly those friendship nights. I also woke up feeling pretty darn great, ready to conquer my days. Now let's not get this confused or start the whispering I was an alcoholic or needed AA meetings. But there was a time I had been known to say, "I like beer!" or "Yes, please, fill it up!" to wine and maybe possibly once or twice finished others' shots when they left them on the table. Seriously, the true wonder was, why on earth would my friends leave a fun-named shot unattended on a table?

I don't pretend to be anything I'm not.
Except for sober, I've pretended to be sober a few times!
—Unknown

After one group night out, I texted out to all the next morning, bright and early, "I feel great! I like water!" Of course, the majority of the responses, many hours later, ranged from "I need water!" to "I should have had water!" Yes, at the time, I felt I was going to be a trendsetter until, well, this mama wanted to party and said, "Yes, please fill her way up!" I did good. The goal was achieved for six months. Five months, three weeks, longer than anyone thought it could be. Yep, once again, go me!

Go ahead set your goals and see what you can achieve. Many things change in this roller coaster of a ride through the years, and now having an adult beverage or five is not much of a thought for me. Therefore, such a goal to conquer would be a breeze. But it certainly brings back some fun memories, and I can't stop laughing and shaking my head that this was once a hiccup to overcome.

One summer, I was giddy with all my plans at the time for my future sister-in-law's bridal shower—a girly party. I showed Ryan the wine glasses I painted, the photo for the veil-cowboy hat I was going to make, the detailed place setting cards, the liquor punch recipe with mint leaves from my garden, the table decoration designs, and the tissue paper balls to hang all around the house. I was just beaming from ear to ear with excitement. What a great party it will be! He looks at me blank and says "I'm so glad I have a penis" and walks away. Men, they just don't get it. And I was surrounded by them!

The night before the Ida-Grovian's arrive for the well-planned bridal shower and dual bachelorette/bachelor party, our life-is-a-party Ethan decided to have quite the little shindig of his own, consisting of football players and their girlfriends. We had been up every two hours, checking doors, windows, and taking note of who was all still at the house. I wasn't miffed but a bit giggly at six in the morning as I was picking up after them because I was pretty sure our upcoming shindig would be a much bigger mess due to many more years of experience, and Ethan would be the

JB for cleanup. Love paybacks! Being a parent can be pretty freaking *awesome* if you play the game right!

Get excited about the little things, set goals for yourself to achieve, try out a new recipe or mixed drink, and plan silly parties with your loved ones. Life is short. Get out, enjoy, and just have a scotch, followed with much-needed water!

I Am a Princess... Didn't You See the Tiara?

Ultimately, it's up to Mom to keep it all together.
On those days when you're just plain tired of
having to be the responsible one, wear a little
something to remember just how special you are.

—Mom

This was my mother's wise advice to me in the early years of earning the title of a working mom: "Wear bright colors on days you are down, wear blah colors on days you feel anxious or agitated." So yes, my wardrobe consists of sequins, bling, and fun animal prints to black, blah, and black.

It was not uncommon to have me sitting at a baseball, football, or some other ball event sporting big bling earrings. It wasn't for you, folks. I'm not trying to impress anyone. Sometimes a girl just needs a little helpful bling-dazzling friend hanging from the lobes! Even today as I sit unshowered, with fresh PJs on, I'm wearing my dangling, blinged earrings. Remember that the next time you see a sister in the pack. Maybe instead of whispering behind her back, go up and give a sisterly hug. Just move on in and give that big ole mama bear a hug. We all need them from time to time. I will make it a goal to do more of that for others! Wished I had done that more in the past.

Looking back, not sure how it had happened, but I had been recruited to walk in the Iowa State Fair parade one summer. We were going to represent Evan's dance studio. Anyone who knows me or this parade would know this was quite the undertaking and had possibly dropped their jaw wondering how on earth this was going to play out for me. Well, after realizing there is no way out of it and I need to step up, I took off my heels and dusted off those styling new tennies that simply looked amazing on my shoe rack. I also informed all parties around me, "Do not be surprised if I curl up in a fetal position halfway through this walk, begging for a glass of wine. Just step over me and march on." Obviously, I survived and have not been taking calls from that gal again! Kidding. We had a good time, a lot of laughs, little sweat, and many aches and pains in muscles I didn't know I had. Just for the record: been there, done that, won't *ever* do again. But I'm certainly glad I gave it a good ole try. It's good to step out of your norm from time to time. The following year, Ryan and I sat all cozy in this super cool jazz bar at the end of the route. We saw just enough of the parade to feel the excitement!

Two months into the boys' seventh- and ninth-grade year of school, we were full force into our careers, working extended hours, yet flexible around the boys' activities. We were running from the moment the alarm went off in the morning to the moment we crashed into bed at night and loving every minute of it. By then we had scaled back on volunteer work and concentrated on our family. Our main focus was making sure we were there for our boys and the furbabies. In this time of running, we had realized that our housekeeping had gone to the wayside. This was frustrating and embarrassing for two super neat people who took the duties as a dual partnership. But still, it was looking pretty bad. When my Ryan said the sweetest, most romantic, what every gal going into their seventeenth year of marriage would want to hear, "Go ahead and sign us up for a cleaning service." OMG. I love him more with the mention of those words than the vows on our wedding day! With this service, it was revealed we would get a deep cleaning at the start. Six to eight hours of digging into every crevice of our home, under every piece of furniture, and on top of every surface. It dawned on me at that moment: running into this cleaning person in a public setting will be far more humiliating than running into my gynecologist or that "urine study in my crotch" gal. I got over that feeling very quickly. It also may have crossed my mind a time or two to sit around in a prom dress, dance costume, or my wedding dress while sipping on a glass of wine while this service was being performed. I should have asked my nieces for a tiara to complete my look. Really, isn't that what every princess does?

Find what makes you happy, what makes you feel good, and strut your stuff. Let people do what they need to do to get there. Isn't that what life is about? To enjoy and just be happy?

Save a Tree

One man's trash is another man's treasure.
—Yotam Ottolenghi

Hug a tree. Just do it. Help be a part of saving the earth. Reduce, reuse, and recycle. Come on, stop being so trashy! Reinvent a jar or reuse a cool whip container. Live simply and make do. Share with others if you don't need, want, or desire your crap anymore. Others may find it useful or turn your thought of junk into a treasure. We have all struggled and abused this from time to time, but at some point in our lives, we wake up and see the bigger picture. You care for your body. You care for others. Care for Mother Earth too. Teach your kids to recycle. Teach your kids to plant and care for a tree. Take back cans and bottles or donate them to a local group doing a can drive. Most importantly, *don't litter!* Personally, I feel if an individual abuses this, we shall stop with the tickets and fines that could easily be paid for and lesson forgotten. Let's start chaining folks to a good old oak in a tight embrace. Public humiliation usually does the job with a lasting impression. Enough said here. Thanks for letting me vent. Do your part!

It's Really Not How You See It—Sometimes

Open your eyes and see all the possibilities!

Sitting at my fifteen-year class reunion, catching up with old high school friends, minding my own business, my first ever boyfriend from way back in grade school walked up to me. Of course, that relationship, if you would call it that at that age, maybe lasted a few months. More likely only a few weeks. But at the time and looking back, he was my boyfriend of my grade school years even though he wouldn't swing with me at recess and would rather play football with his buddies. I'm over it, kind of, roll of the eyes. Boys and their damn balls! Anyway, back on track. He walked up to me. It was obvious from the glassy red eyes he had one to eight adult drinks too many. (Been there, no judgment here. He must like beer too!) He opened up on his feelings for me while in high school. Now it wasn't a one-line confession but a repeated, over-and-over, growing louder, "alcohol truth serum" confession. He claimed I was so cool and had this cool boyfriend that he couldn't even approach me for fear of rejection. Stop the truck. What? The witnesses and I sat there, shocked, blank stares, followed by nervous, awkward air laughs. We all looked at one another to make sure we were seeing and hearing the same scene going down in front of us as more started staring in our direction, all while his wife was in the corner and my Ryan was sitting across the room, chatting it up with another hubby. I felt embarrassed by the odd attention and numb with shock, thinking *me*? His tucked-in, collared shirt with a belt tribe never looked at me nor talked to me in high school. I was in a way different group. We marched to our own beat, we wore odd clothing, and therefore we stuck to our own too. While he was still going on in his confession, I quickly jumped to the conclusion and stared angrily. (Oh snap! The dragon is about to come out!) "Are you making fun of me?" Not letting him respond, I quickly followed up with, "You are, you're making fun of me!" He, in all his honest drunkenness, looked shocked and assured me he was not. One friend whispered, "I think he's meaning this sincerely." Apparently, he honestly had these feelings. The adult drink and many moons later of not seeing each other gave him an opportunity to let it out. Also, remember, I still looked like that teenage girl staring in the bathroom mirror so many years ago, right? I have to admit, I was embarrassed and flattered. You see, folks, with a rude awakening, I realized in a more mature time, we may have interpreted things all wrong. How old situations and feelings appeared to us may not have been the actual way things were. Open your eyes and look around. You may see your peers in a whole different light. And it's perfectly okay to step out of your norm and talk to someone you normally would not think you had any business too.

What may had appeared to some that I had it all together, for me, it was a wonder how I ever made it to work every day. It was a wonder how I had kept a pet, plant, or a kid alive. It was a wonder how I held a job or even helped run a company. One working day I had put on a dress to show a little leg. I remembered to shave but not to lotion. I thought, *Eh, when I got to my office, I will lotion up.* After two meetings, an appointment, and several hours into the day, I still was lacking lotion, and it was bugging me something awful. As always, I was into multitasking, digging through the piles on my desk while reading an email. I had reached into my drawer to grab the many MaryKay Satin Hands samples I had thrown in there. I grabbed, ripped apart, squirted into my hands, and globbed onto my legs all while still reading an email. I'm trying to rub vigorously and fast so no one walks into my office, all while forgetting MaryKay Satin Hands does not only consist of lotion but a gritty scrub as well. Yep, you guessed it. I had fully exfoliated my legs, in my office, at work, with the door wide open. After having a laughing fit at my desk, with my head down and several white sand particles all over me, I grabbed the correct packet and had *finally moisturized my damn legs* with less than two hours left in my working day. No spa appointment needed for me after work, mission accomplished! I was a seasoned, multitasking, working mom. Hear me roar!

One year I had found the love for coconut oil for about everything: lotion, hair smoother, deodorant. I was trying to go as natural as possible. It had a faint scent only desirable to the furbabies. But this one particular work morning, I just couldn't take it any longer. I needed a girly scent, although

I had run out of a lovely spa scented oil earlier in the week. I was doing what all us stretched-thin mothers do, making do until we ran errands on the coming Saturday. Looking at my options in the house, germ spray for my son's sport bag or a dryer static sheet just wasn't going to cut it. So like any other clever mother, I rubbed a favorite Scentsy bar all over my skin and my clothes. Why not? Smells awesome in the air. After many hours of sporting the nice scent, I can assure you I did not get a rash or strange looks from anyone in my sniff zone. So lesson of the month, when you find yourself in a bind, rub away with a Scentsy bar. I approve this busy mom cleverness! (*Disclaimer*: I cannot be sued for this if you try and receive a rash, because you are an idiot taking advice from an obviously delirious, wine-drinking, sleep-deprived working mother of teenage boys.)

Only in the Timm house do we get on these subjects. One summer before the boys' seventh- and ninth-grade year of school, the boys, including my Ryan, informed me that on top of not hearing well, I may tend to come across unapproachable when I'm deep in thought or sitting neutral—that sometimes I have bitchy resting face. Apparently, there's quite the joke among them how I'm perceived by others who have no idea of my hearing issues or of my terribly busy squirrel mind. The boys added they were going to place a stamp on my forehead: *Welcome*! (They are so ornery.) Most of my friends and family are loud talkers and know to get my attention before talking. In fact, one gal was a thigh slapping "Jenn!" There had been many times people had mentioned to them that I had snubbed them, when actually I had no idea they were even talking to me! Yep, she's a dragon, therefore a snob too. I'll be honest, most of the time this hard-of-hearing gal was on a roller coaster ride of thoughts far, far away, with the oh so nice, bitchy resting face syndrome going on. I'm so glad I could bring humor to my boys with this wonderful combination.

I also smiled a lot or changed subjects when I had no idea what people had said, and I was frankly just too tired and frustrated of asking "what?" It can all be exhausting. Another lovely laugh, and most of my friends and family joked that I come across stoned as well. I assure you, I was not. I could have a surgery to have implants, but you can only have one done at a time, and it takes up to one year of remapping the sounds. I'm not that committed to hearing, people. Did you know the majority of insurances don't even cover hearing loss or hearing aids? They will cover only if it was caused from a car accident. Trust me, Ryan has offered several times to slam me into a wall with our vehicle to avoid writing another five-year check to replace my hearing aids. To this date, I'm on my fifth set of hearing aids. I could have had an amazing boob job, tummy tuck, face-lift, etc., for what has been sitting in my ears through the years. Okay, that doesn't interest me either, but you get the point. After seeing the large dollar signs accompanying the implant surgery, I decided, eh, it's not worth hearing everyone that much. Or if I do decide to have the surgery, I will start charging my peers if they want me to listen to them. What do you feel the going rate per word shall be? I'm debating, possibly charging more for annoying voices. I have a handful of people already flagged for that list. So for now, I'll keep with the hearing aids. I do better in close settings; therefore, I shall become a hermit in my later years and quite possibly just go without them. Now you all know.

I'm not shy or avoiding, maybe a bit moody, frustrated, or distracted. But mostly I didn't hear you nor feel like trying to figure out what you had just said to me for the umpteenth time. And quite frankly, it just makes the whole greeting awkward for all parties. It's exhausting being hard of hearing, and some days I just simply don't want to play the game. Sorry, not sorry.

On the plus side, we found humor in our situation a few times. If anyone had ever seen Ryan and I in a movie theater before the days of Bluetooth hearing headsets offered, you would have witnessed Ryan talking in my ear, replaying the movie. It probably looked like we were necking the entire time. Oh, the rumors. Yep, that's Ethan and Evan's parents. Giggle, giggle!

Just breathe. Learn to laugh at your situations, learn to see things from a different view, learn to shake your head with a big grin, learn to shrug your shoulders and say, "Oh well, it is what it is." It is a good life and what you make it to be!

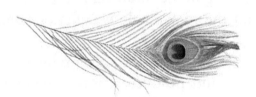

At the beginning and all through this ride, the pull was to create and create, I did. It may have not been on a path once envisioned as a naive schoolgirl. But I do realize I did create the ultimate masterpiece. For me, it was with my Ryan, Ethan Douglas, Evan Dennis, and our awesome, one hell of a ride!

About the Author

Jennifer Collins-Timm recently left the workforce as a regional sales Manager to enjoy more Zen time—Jenn time at her home, with her husband, Ryan. As her two Timm boys are gearing up on their own adventures as young adults, she is now a proud stay-at-home dog mom to her four beloved furbabies on The Zen Ranch. She spends her days planning home improvement projects, enlightening others on the remarkable benefits of pure CBD oil*, and creating her next book.

Jennifer writes her stories based off her unconventional yet resourceful and productive way of handling motherhood and life in general with sarcasm and laugh-out-loud moments. Plus, her Timm men give her great material to work with!

*www.JennHempAlive.com